Tools and Fuels

How Catholic Teachers Can Become Saints, Beat Burnout and Save the World

Jonathan E Doyle

Published by Choicez Media GPO Box 2745, Tuggeranong, ACT 2940, Australia
www.choicez.com.au

ISBN 978-0-9775315-4-7

Printed in the United States of America.

Acknowledgments:
A big thanks to Andy Mullins, Tim Hawkes, Romina Mandrini and Sandra Bejjani for editing and proofing the manuscript. To Jeanine Doyle for the cover artwork and Michelle Donaldson for typesetting.

Dedication

I want to dedicate this book to all those many thousands of Catholic teachers and principals who have always felt they were doing it alone, and to the many fine Catholic educators who deeply desire to serve God and the Church He established. You may be hidden and you may often wonder if what you're doing makes a difference…it does! Your tireless service of young people and your love of the faith inspires me and makes me want to keep telling this story for as long as I am able.

Contents

Introduction

I remember the exact moment I realized that the lunatics were running the asylum.

I was standing in a large room in a large city. We had just finished our first-ever day-long seminar for our new business. One hundred and fifty teenage students at a Catholic school in Melbourne, Australia had just spent a day with us exploring the new vision for sexual decision-making and relationships found in Pope John Paul II's *Theology of the Body*. I'll explain what happened in that room in a moment. But first, let me set the stage.

I had come from a background in Catholic high school teaching and Karen had been a nurse. I loved young people but the system had worn me down so quickly. I remember when my resignation letter hit my first principal's desk. He looked up and said, "I just don't understand this!" All I could think was, "Really? You really don't understand this?" I had given two hundred percent to my kids. I really cared about them but I quickly sensed that the entire system itself was unsustainable. How could we stay creative under such pressures? Why did so few staff want to meet for any kind of prayer or spiritual formation? Why was career progression linked to time served rather than effort expended or results produced? Why were so many of the teachers around me exhausted or cynical? Why did many of them seem deeply disconnected to the Catholic faith that was supposed to sustain and empower them as missionaries to children and young people?

We were married several weeks into the first term of my first year as a new teacher. Interesting times. I only lasted another year at that school. My subversive ideas about what it meant to be a

Catholic teacher meant I was truly a square peg trying to fit with a spectacular lack of success into a round hole. I could not let go of the idea that there was something very special about Catholic education, about young people, about faith and how all those things could potentially intersect in powerful ways. I seemed to sense intuitively that as Catholic schools, and the teachers in them, drifted further and further from the faith and mission that was at the heart of all we were supposed to be doing, then things were going to get a lot worse. As a result, a few weeks later, Karen and I took up an offer to go and work at a boarding school in the remote north of Australia.

Living and working with so many young people of both sexes meant that we saw up close and personal their challenges, hopes and sufferings. We wanted to do something about it. We knew we couldn't help all of them, but we did not let that stop us from wanting to help some of them. I'd already finished a Master of Education and after eighteen months we decided to leave the boarding school, relocate and both enroll in another master's program at the John Paul II Pontifical Institute for Studies on Marriage and the Family in Melbourne. I'm all for passion and enthusiasm but let's not be silly about it. If we combined that passion and enthusiasm with a deep formation in Catholic philosophical anthropology, personalism and Thomistic studies, then I figured we'd be downright unstoppable!

So we left the tropical north to study some more. We started driving. We thought it would be romantic. We were wrong. On a car journey of over fifteen hundred miles, I think the romance ended somewhere about mile five. We set up a tent near a bend in the highway. It was still brutally hot at 2 am and every truck coming either way lit the place up like a disco. Ah, the sweet sound of a semi-trailer's compression braking as you slowly dehydrate! The next night we stayed in a five-star resort.

Since then, I have a simple rule. I only camp in places where you can order 24-hour room service, and since no place with a campsite has offered that service to date, the cupboard is thankfully bare of camping memories. Thank you, Jesus!

Meanwhile, the time at the Pontifical Institute changed our lives. You know those rare moments you have a few times in your life when you are suddenly confronted with authentic truth, beauty or goodness? They don't come often, but if you're open, they change you. I remember sitting in a lecture room at the Institute listening to Monsignor Livio Melina, one of the best moral theologians in the world. I really liked him. He told me over coffee that it could, theoretically, be morally licit to own a Porsche. That made me like him more. Karen said I made it up, but he really did!

At one point, as he spoke about the nature of human love, I suddenly had the most profound sense of being in the presence of truth. Not in the presence of an opinion or a theory, but in the presence of an explanation of reality that resonated on the experiential, affective and spiritual plane. I *knew* he was right. I knew at that moment that there were truths that were genuinely transcendental because they transcended any individual experience. They were universal. They conformed to reality. Or, rather, reality conformed to them. It was confronting. I was changed by that moment in ways that carry me these years later.

So this study is what led, in a roundabout way, to standing in front of 150 students that first day. Admiral Grace Hopper is credited with saying that if you have a good idea you should just go ahead and do it because it's always easier to ask for forgiveness than it is to ask for permission. I realized very quickly that the work we wanted to do with and for young people was not going to happen under a standard schooling model. We were not going to get that type of permission. Few schools, if any, would see it as core business.

So what did we do? Well, if you can still remember the famous Remington shaver TV commercials with Victor Kiam saying, *"I liked it so much, I bought the company!"* I guess our approach to John Paul II and Catholicism in general was that we liked it all so much we wanted to *start* a company! So that's what we did. We figured that if the message was good enough then we could build a business that actually solved problems and helped people.

As I sit here writing these words, I have already spoken around the world to well over 300,000 people. However, that day with those students was our first-ever live seminar. Praise God, we nailed it. It was such a positive experience. We felt vindicated on a few levels. We knew that young people were capable of responding to what I called *telling a better story*. We helped them perceive an attractive narrative about what could be possible for their lives. They were moved, challenged and responsive. There was no cynicism. At least not from the students.

As the day finished, many students came up to talk and thank us for the message. And then it happened. I ended up talking to the Deputy Principal. I can still see him clearly. He was clutching a clipboard to his chest with folded arms. We made some small talk and then he said the words I've never forgotten: *"Well, that was not too bad, but I guess the main thing to remember is that this is just one story, it's our story, but it's just one story."* Effectively he was saying that a solid, authentic and compelling presentation of the Catholic Church's teaching on human love and relationship was *just a story.*

I don't know about you, but the minute I hear a Catholic mention the word *story* I know it's only a few moments until we hear the word *journey*. When I hear *story* and *journey*, I know I am about to be sucked into an inextricable vortex of post-modern Catholic psychobabble. When someone suggests that we are "just sharing our story," you know that they most likely triple majored in post-modern relativism where Catholicism is just one more menu choice on the all-you-can-eat buffet of post-millennial spiritual questing. This was the exact moment I realized that the lunatics were running the asylum. Why?

This guy was directly responsible for the pastoral care of twelve hundred young people. Twelve hundred mostly baptized Catholics whose parents, with exceptions, were at least clinging to the vague idea that the school may, perhaps, reinforce at some level the parents' faith perspective. But the truth was that he simply didn't believe it. Who knows exactly what his faith position was. Whatever it was, it wasn't Catholic. It was not Catholic in the sense that being Catholic means holding to the basic tenets of a two thousand-year-old magisterium or being in accord with the Bishop of Rome. You don't have to pray a rosary every day to be on the team, but at least some alignment with the basic tenets of the faith would be nice.

However, I am grateful for the window it opened in my mind and the questions it raised. *What happens in a Catholic school when people begin to see Catholicism as just one option among many? What happens in a Catholic school when the faith becomes less and less relevant?* Or, you could ask the question the other way. *What happens in a Catholic school when the staff and leadership have a deep and vibrant faith that informs all aspects of their practice?* You see, one way or another you end up with a certain kind of school. People think it's about the money, the funding, the socio-economic demographic, the pedagogy. It's not. Damien of Molokai transformed lives and saved souls with zero funding. Teresa of Calcutta reached the world by washing the bodies of strangers. We see *what* they did but we often overlook *why* they did it and, I think, most importantly, it was the *why* that sustained them.

I'm a realist. I left that school knowing we had done all we could on that given day. But I also knew that the likelihood of the message we shared being reinforced was minimal. Pastorally and sacramentally, there was little chance these sheep were going to be fed in the way they needed over the long term. The shepherds were off duty.

This is not a book about blame. We inhabit a social and political milieu of victims and shrill voices of rage and anger. I am old enough to realize that this gets us nowhere. Interestingly, each night this week I have been reading my young daughter Dale Carnegie's famous book *How To Win Friends and Influence People*. The first chapter highlights the truth that criticism just doesn't work. When you criticize people they just shut down or push back. I understand that carefully structured feedback and evaluation can help people grow and change, but outright criticism just doesn't work. However, it's hard not to criticize, isn't it? I get so darn frustrated at times. I'm sure you also see many things, either in your work or the wider world, that drive you crazy! I love my faith and I love the Catholic Church and I love Catholic education and all the heroic Catholic educators who are out there trying to make a difference. However, I also get so frustrated by the failures, accommodations and cowardice that we often see. But I guess the task of this book is to keep focused on both the "what's possible" and who the real enemy is. We need to fight the right enemy. It's always the same enemy – he just uses different tactics at different moments in history.

So, why did I share that story with you about the first seminar we ever did? It's simply because I was confronted by the fact that the person who was leading didn't really believe in the very core reason for the existence of the school. It would be like a US Marine who did not believe in patriotism or defending their country, or a professional athlete who wasn't that interested in winning. You see, a Catholic school is not like any other place. It emerged in history for a very particular purpose. The further we drift from that purpose, from the very core that sustains it, the worse things become. It's a slow process of atrophy. Nothing falls apart rapidly. As we drift, we become teachers with a *job* rather than saints in the making. The real deal is that we are charged by God to be missionaries and visible angels, as Don Bosco used to say, in the lives of young people.

An easily observable sociological principle is that organizations and groups that deeply value their internal narrative, their *reason for existence*, tend to be stronger and more effective. The best companies also tend to be those with the strongest founding ideals, mission and internal culture. We value this in business but many schools seem unsure about how to apply it to their own self-understanding. Perhaps pluralism, relativism and post-modernism have convinced many Catholics that to be vibrantly or passionately Catholic is to be non-inclusive or disrespectful. It seems many of us don't want to be *too* Catholic because we are worried that people will think we are religious fundamentalists or zealots.

There are, of course, many great teachers who try hard to pass on the faith but, like Jesus, did not come for the healthy. This is not so much a book for the ones out there giving it their all. This is for all of us "in between." This is for all of us getting burned out. This is for all of us who have forgotten that it's way more than a job. This is for that spark way down inside you that really wants your life to count for something. This is for the part of you that wants to fall over the finish line and hear a voice say, "Well done, good and faithful servant."

This is a book about what's possible. It's also a book about why things aren't working. It's a book about a hope that I can't let go of. I can tell you, I never chose this mission. This mission chose me. And I think, if you've read this far, there is a good chance that you didn't choose teaching, but that teaching, or the God behind the teaching, chose you. There are zero coincidences in the kingdom of God. I try to get every teacher to realize that the same sovereign God who holds the universe together is so interested in the minute details of your life that He knew this would be the vocation perfectly suited to you. Even with its many challenges and hardships, He knew you could do this.

I want to share with you what I have seen in Catholic schools around the world. I want to tell you that burnout and exhaustion and cynicism and school closures do not have to be our default experiences and fallback position. I'm a kind of charge-the-machine-guns kind of guy. I think that we need to find our confidence again and go back into the world. The world needs us. The world needs *you* to live your vocation and be the Catholic teacher you were called to be. You have a vocation. You don't have a job. I want to show you the one irrefutable way that you can not only survive teaching, but thrive. I want to show you that your vocation is not just about your students – it's very much about you and about how God wants to use teaching to make you a saint. No, really! I mean it.

The definition of insanity is doing the same thing over and over again while expecting a different result.

– Albert Einstein

Chapter 1

The Real Problem

I have a friend who is a global business consultant. He makes a bucket of cash by doing one thing really, really well – he asks the right questions. He has a bunch of lackeys who then do all the fancy graphs and diagnostics and implement all the strategic stuff. He just asks the right questions. He taught me a long time ago that most of his work is simply about digging deep enough to uncover what the *real* problem is by asking the right questions. Asking the right questions always leads to solving the right problem. This matters because it's highly possible for extremely intelligent people to spend lots of time doing all sorts of fancy things, but addressing the wrong problem.

Making the right diagnosis of a problem allows you to deploy the most effective strategy for dealing with it. Many years ago, Karen was diagnosed with a tumor in the pituitary gland. Pretty freaky time of our lives, really. Lots of worry. Lots of stress. It came from nowhere. One day she was fine and the next day she had extreme headaches and could not tolerate the light.

What followed was a month in hospital where the doctors tried to find the cause of the problem. They asked many questions, just not the right questions. She was sent home in a worse state than when she was admitted and with an inaccurate diagnosis of an unexplained migraine.

She became progressively worse. The next morning I was able to get her into a private hospital where they accurately diagnosed the cause of the headaches. A tumor, which had looked benign on the CT scan, had actually had a small haemorrhage.

After a few more tests and a procedure she was discharged. We were referred to a number of specialists to follow up on the best course of action.

Over a few weeks we ended up seeing a brain surgeon, a neurologist and an endocrinologist. Each of them had lots of certificates on the wall and nice leather chairs. Based on the same information provided to them all, these were the responses we got:

Brain surgeon: "I can operate next week if you'd like me to."

Neurologist: "I'm not really sure what we should do."

Endocrinologist: "Whatever you do, don't let anyone with a scalpel anywhere near you."

I love how the brain surgeon said "if you'd like me to." I mean, really? This guy is the person who hacks into people's skulls and he is leaving it up to us? Nice! I was sort of looking for a larger display of self-confidence on his part. At least the neurologist was honest enough to admit he was clueless. Personally, though, I really liked the endocrinologist. He was both professorial and a straight-shooter, and clearly no fan of brain surgeons.

The point here is that three "experts" were offering different solutions to one problem. There were not three tumors – only one. Surgery could have been wrong and doing nothing could have been wrong. In the end, the tumor and the haemorrhage miraculously shrunk so we'll never know, but I hope you get my point. We need to really *know* the problem to be able to accurately provide the right solution. So what exactly is the real problem?

For me, something is not working when most of our students leave our schools without any real sense of faith. For me, something is wrong when many of our teachers just don't care that deeply about the faith. For me, something is wrong when so many good teachers become burned out, cynical and exhausted.

One of the most poignant moments of my staff seminars was sharing some data on the impact of faith formation efforts on our students. When I was doing my first master's degree, I read some data from a twenty-five-year study of Catholic high school students in one large state. The researcher's follow-up of students suggested that within the first twelve months after graduation, less than five percent of graduates set foot inside a church. *Less than five percent!*

The counter-argument, of course, is that getting kids to go to church is not the sole responsibility of Catholic schools. I agree. There are many factors at play. There is the witness and faith practice of parents, wider social influences, and more. However, let's be clear on two points. First, the catechism makes it abundantly clear that the Eucharist is "the source and summit of the faith." Second, most students spend about fifteen years with us in Catholic education.

If the Eucharist is the source and summit of the Catholic faith, and we have fifteen years to help develop that faith but we don't, then something is wrong. Terribly wrong.

To be blunt, in many of our schools we have to face the truth: nothing we have said or done or witnessed in fifteen years has been compelling enough for students to take a sacramental relationship with Jesus Christ seriously. I don't want to face God with that on my conscience, I really don't. We have to be bold enough to say that our students don't believe it because many people responsible for Catholic schools simply don't believe or practice it. Many of our students will go on to love football because our schools loved it and we loved it and, yes, because our culture reinforced it. However, it's fair to say that most of us tend to be more passionate about football than about the real presence of Jesus Christ made manifest on the altar.

I try to make the uncomfortable point in my seminars that we simply would not tolerate in any other sphere of life the outcomes we see in the faith formation and Christian discipleship of young people. For example, businesses exist to create value, produce profit for shareholders and, increasingly, make some sort of contribution to the common good. If a business stops creating profit or value, that business is wiped out. If it is a big business, then shareholder meetings tend to get pretty heated when performance is below what's required. No one tolerates poor performance for long in business.

It's the same in professional sports, the arts and politics. Once we identify poor performance in the core goals of a team, dance company or political party, forces begin to move to create change. Strangely, the education space (or, for our purpose, the Catholic education space) seems to be a place where goals are not really clear and very little, if anything, is done when the goals are missed. If our goal is to help young people encounter Jesus Christ and become His disciples while also developing their human, academic, artistic and sporting potential, then what happens when we miss these goals? Who is held accountable? What do we consider changing?

These days, when academic performance drops we have a super-responsive canary in the coal mine. It's called aspirational parenting. Many parents have also lost sight of the fundamental nature and purpose of Catholic education. They are focused upon academic success. When grades drop they act quickly and decisively. They email the principal, they make appointments with teachers, they change schools, they light up social media and start talking with other parents.

But who makes any noise about a lack of spiritual formation? Pretty much no one. If the primary, though not exclusive, aim of Catholic education is an encounter with Jesus and no one is encountering Jesus, then we have an epic mission fail. It's the emperor's new clothes. It's like Ford not making any cars and expecting to stay in business, or an NFL team hoping no one will notice if they don't score a single touchdown all season. Ford makes cars. NFL teams play football. Catholic education helps young people encounter Jesus – or at least that's what it says in all those pretty mission statements that no one actually reads.

I may offend a lot of people. It's not my intention, but I've had a privileged position in witnessing much of what is happening in Catholic education around the world, and we need to wake up. We need to ask ourselves some really tough questions about what our schools are really for. We need to ask ourselves some tough questions about what our *lives* are for. We need to ask ourselves what vocation *really* means.

I don't know about you but I am not a huge fan of failure. To be accurate, I am not a fan of failing the same way over and over again. Someone once said, "It's okay to make mistakes, but try to make sure they are new ones." If we keep failing at the same core mission tasks over and over again, then something is up.

Let's be fair, there is a load of good will. It's not as if Catholic teachers around the world are wanting to fail. I think it's that they are simply not being given enough information, evangelization and encouragement. So let's dig deeper into what's really happening and what we can do about it. What we need first is to get very clear on *exactly* what the mission of Catholic education is all about.

All great human endeavors begin with an aim.

Chapter 2

The Mission of Catholic Education

My brother would have made a brilliant military historian. Bookish by nature, he must have read almost everything published on just about every conflict you can think of. When I was a surly teenager, he used to take me off-road driving in his 4WD exploring the nearby mountains. He could talk for hours about everything from Gettysburg to Pearl Harbor and Thermopylae to the Zulu Wars of the 19th century. I would throw in the occasional question and off he'd go again. I found it therapeutic, the low hum of the diesel and the banquet of ideas, people and moments frozen in time.

I remember him once talking about one of his favorite books on the great generals of history. It was kind of a distillation of the unifying principles that saw many of the great leaders develop their legends. Among the core ideas was something that always stayed in my mind: *selection and maintenance of aim.* It's a central idea in military leadership. Step one, carefully select what it is that you are aiming to accomplish. Step two, don't deviate from pressing toward that aim. It is important to know what you are trying to do, but it is just as important to not let yourself become distracted. It is crucial to maintain the aim.

All great human endeavors begin with an aim. Steve Jobs said his goal was to "put a dent in the universe." Martin Luther King had his dream. The Marines are "always faithful" and the Girl Scouts are always "prepared." In Aristotle's *Ethics*, he begins Book 1 by stating that all human action is motivated toward some good, some desired state of being that is perceived as better than the current state. We are the type of beings that always seek, for better or worse, to aim toward *something*. Sometime between the 10th and 6th centuries BC, the writer of the Book of Proverbs was telling us that "without vision the people perish."

The Truth About Our Mission

To say that the mission of Catholic education is failing is a bold statement. Many will disagree. It will depend on what we think the mission is. Marcellin Champagnat, the French founder of the Marist Brothers, said that he wanted his schools to turn out "good Christians and good citizens." He knew what he was trying to do. Recently, I was asked to spend a week speaking to staff in a large diocese. A senior person in the diocese sent me some talking points about what they wanted me to cover. The notes included the following statement:

> *"Whatever our role is in Catholic education, it is first and foremost to accompany children to choose a full and meaningful life."*

Umm...where do we start with that? Let's begin by parsing it a little. The embedded philosophy here is that the most important thing we do in Catholic education is to "accompany" children to choose a full and meaningful life. Really? I get the whole John 10:10 inference, but I'm just not sure the language is helpful. I mean, a psychologist or counselor could help a young person choose a full and meaningful life. A couple of YouTube videos might be enough to help a young person choose a full and meaningful life.

Jesus made it pretty clear that if you gain the entire world but lose your soul, then you still lose. If you have a full and meaningful life but reject relationship with God, then you lose. We have a therapeutic culture so deeply embedded in maximizing positive feeling states that we are forever losing sight of what actually matters. We don't succeed in Catholic education because students live full and meaningful lives as their exclusive goal. That sounds outrageous and it even feels strange to type it. The deeper truth is that we win in Catholic education when students end up living full and meaningful lives *because* they became disciples of Jesus Christ, found a home in His Church, and went on to discover and develop their unique gifts and vocation in service of the world.

I like paradigm shifts and metaphors. I like the way that a simple statement, image or story can shift how we think. In a sound bite culture we are increasingly sensitized to consuming information in smaller and smaller doses. Knowing this, I always share a favorite insight when I talk with Catholic educators about mission.

Pope Paul VI wrote an encyclical document called *Evangelii Nuntiandi*, which roughly translates as *The Attempt to Proclaim the Gospel to the People of Our Time.* I like Paul VI. He always looks serene when you see pictures of him. How is it that the guy looked serene when running the global Church and I never look serene running after three children? Anyway...he had a powerful quote in this magnificent document, where he stated:

> *"The Catholic Church does not have a mission. She is a mission."*

Boom! That is what I call Papal smackdown! I love those words. So simple yet so subversive of all our paradigms about what the Catholic Church is and what Catholic education is all about.

The problem we face in Catholic education is that most of us think that *mission* is some kind of religious thingy that got tacked onto schools as an afterthought. Mission is not something that Catholic schools *do*. Mission is something that Catholic schools *are*. They exist as an integral part of the mission that *is* the Catholic Church. Apart from this mission there is zero, nil, *nada*, zilch reason for Catholic schools to exist. Any form of government or private education will suffice to allow people to take up a place in society.

We have to get this. We have to get it soon. The world needs us to get this. We have to understand that apart from the Catholic Church and the mission that the Catholic Church *is*, we have no reason for existence.

So what exactly is this mission? What exactly is the Catholic Church doing in history? Why has it outlived every temporal power? Beyond the glory of the Vatican, the beauty of the liturgy, the sacraments and incense...what is actually going on? Why does it exist?

Thankfully, Jesus himself made this part clear. First, he told Peter that He was going to build a Church and that Peter would be the rock on which it was built and, importantly, He also told Peter that even the very gates of hell would not hold out against the Church. Second, when Jesus was about to ascend to the Father, He made it clear that His disciples had one single task. They were to go out to the whole world and make new disciples. That's it. He didn't tell them to start schools, hold fundraisers and make sure that kids could get into good colleges. All of that is fine and we'll get to it in a moment, but for now let's focus on the basics.

The Church and Catholic education do not *have* a mission. They *are* a mission. And that mission is to do exactly what Jesus said, which is to make disciples. If we are not making disciples then we are failing in the mission. It's that simple. People might choke on their cornflakes and many people who are too heavily invested in the status quo or too spiritually dead to care will try to make it about something else. They are wrong. I am sick of seeing so many sophists masquerading as "educational thought leaders" who want to make this way more complex than it needs to be. When you hear long sentences with long words about best practice and 21st-century learners and student-centered pedagogy but nothing about Jesus, then you know they've lost the mission.

For crying out loud, here's the thing about Jesus. When you actually really encounter Him, when you turn your life over to relationship with Him, then your whole life shifts. The axis of your life is inverted. How can you then compartmentalize that into something you do on a Sunday for forty-five minutes? Why were the disciples able to change the world? Seriously, think about this for a moment. A handful of mostly illiterate Hebrews in a cultural backwater of the Roman Empire change the entire course of human history. How did they do that? Simple! They had experienced an encounter with Jesus Christ and this changed their entire life and empowered them to do the impossible. And you, my friend, are no different.

So the first and most crucial thing we have to understand about Catholic education is that it is a place for making disciples of Jesus Christ, our crucified and risen Lord. Anyone who forgets that is going to, at best, retard their own vocational capacity and, at worst, perpetuate our students' reading of us as so uninspired by the Gospel that it must not matter to us. And if it does not matter to us, then it won't matter to them.

Last night I was reading a new book by Archbishop Charles Chaput, and he expresses the same sentiment with just as much force:

> *"The reason the Christian faith doesn't matter to so many of our young people is that – too often – it didn't really matter to us."*

Two Implications

I want to suggest two simple implications of this central focus on mission. First, as I suggest above, if we don't know Jesus we cannot make disciples. You can't give any energy to talking about something you either know nothing about or don't really believe. For example, I don't spend much time on street corners trying to get people to believe in the Easter bunny. In fact, if I started doing that then I'm pretty sure it would be a case of Karen saying something like, "Darling...we need to talk." I don't devote my life to making disciples of the Easter bunny because I don't believe he's real. Sadly, there are too many people working in Catholic schools who either don't really believe Jesus is who He said He is or they act like they don't care either way.

At this point in seminars, I love to share the incredible words of C.S. Lewis on the identity of Jesus:

> *"I am trying here to prevent anyone saying the really foolish thing that people often say about Him: I'm ready to accept Jesus as a great moral teacher, but I don't accept his claim to be God. That is the one thing we must not say. A man who was merely a man and said the sort of things Jesus said would not be a great moral teacher. He would either be a lunatic – on the level with the man who*

> *says he is a poached egg – or else he would be the Devil of Hell. You must make your choice. Either this man was, and is, the Son of God, or else a madman or something worse. You can shut him up for a fool, you can spit at him and kill him as a demon or you can fall at his feet and call him Lord and God, but let us not come with any patronizing nonsense about his being a great human teacher. He has not left that open to us. He did not intend to."*

Lewis wasn't a Catholic, but he sure as hell seems to have a better understanding of the implications of Jesus's claims than a few Catholic principals and leaders I've met. Seriously, think about it for a moment. Jesus claims to be the eternal, consubstantial Son of the Father. He spoke the cosmos into existence with a single word and sustains it by His word. He created you, loved you from all eternity, suffered for you, destroyed the power of death and hell for you, and yet we struggle to live our lives like this is real or something we might want to share. This is the first task of renewing Catholic education. The first task is to renew ourselves or, rather, to seek Him and to allow ourselves to be renewed. My other great mantra is to tell teachers endlessly that we simply cannot give what we do not possess. We cannot live this mission, we cannot make disciples, if we are not disciples ourselves. If we do not know Him, then we cannot make Him known.

The second implication is that we need to repent of this current historical obsession with test results and getting kids into college. We are so afraid of not being academically rigorous. I think what most principals are afraid of is falling enrollments. The internal narrative seems to be that if we don't get high enough test scores, then parents will talk and students will walk!

Our first obsession needs to be Jesus and helping young people to encounter Him by the authentic witness of our lives. We need to have a constant focus on making disciples. We need to have a constant focus on helping every student to encounter the real and living Jesus and finding a home in the Church He founded. Why? Is this about filling the pews? No. It's about the fact that despite all its sins and scandals, the Church is still for so many of us a house of hope and healing and belonging. It's also a place where grace is found in the sacraments and beauty flows from the liturgy, and there is the great consolation and stability of the magisterium and the saints and martyrs and the tens of millions of men and women who have gone before us.

The Essential Filter

In essence, the focus upon mission, upon making disciples, must become what I am calling the *essential filter.* We must begin to ask the tough questions. As I said earlier, we cannot address the challenges we face until we start asking the right questions. *Do I really know Jesus? Am I living and teaching and caring for young people in a way that points them to him?* Jesus must become our filter. Helping young people to know Him must become our essential filter. And, as I will discuss in what's to come, it is this filter that will, in turn, allow us to pursue academic, sporting, artistic or musical excellence for young people.

For too long we have had all this backward. We have put temporal results so far ahead of the original mission. We need to humble ourselves and we need to take a risk. We need to risk that if we put Him first and His call to make disciples, then He will abundantly, above and beyond, meet any needs we have for other outcomes. You see, when you know Jesus and He empowers your vocation, you will see young people differently. You will want the best for them in a new way. You will want to see them flourish because you will slowly, progressively be developing the same heart that Jesus has for them. You will want for them what He wants for them.

It's no coincidence that Jesus said we need to seek first the kingdom of God and His righteousness and then everything else we need will be given to us as well. My central premise, the heartbeat of all I have been doing over the last two decades, is that we have inverted the proper order of our work in Catholic schools. We have tried to please Caesar before we have tried to serve God. If we return to Him, He will return to us. I am convinced that if enough teachers do this, we will truly see a revival in Catholic education.

Integral Formation

Dylan had everything going for him. He was fifteen, athletic and came from a wealthy home with parents who cared. I was his rugby coach in a state-level team. He was good. I was privileged to help make him better.

Joe was from a very broken family in a remote area. He was not athletic. He was overweight and propped up his shattered self-esteem by defiant behavior with most teachers at the school where I was working. Somehow, I found a way to get him to like poetry. I cannot recall what I did, but it worked. He would pronounce the word as "pome" instead of "po-em." Always made me smile. All these years later I have no idea what happened to him.

Does Joe still write poetry? Does Dylan still play rugby? I don't know. However, there is one thing I do know. For the time that I was with both of these students, I was able, as a Catholic teacher, to play some small part in uncovering, affirming and elevating their gifts. And this leads us to the second great part of the mission of Catholic education.

I want to be very clear with you about what I've written here about the formation of disciples in a Catholic school. You may have found my tone strident, too direct, confrontational. I do that because I believe passionately that we have lost our way and lost a sense of the necessary balance in many of our schools. We are running scared and have lost our trust that God will show up for us. I want to be clear that while the formation of disciples, the living of the Gospel by staff and its clear and consistent presentation is crucial to the mission of a Catholic school, it is not the *only* aspect of its mission. Our goal is not to create a cult or some kind of Catholic madrassa. Yes, Jesus is the cornerstone, the foundation, but He has big plans for us. More than we can ask, hope or imagine.

After years of speaking in schools around the world, and years writing content for our online formation program, Going Deeper, I began to learn more about the core foundations that make up a great Catholic school. After the core focus upon Jesus and the making of disciples, we come to the rather sonorous phrase integral formation.

You have been doing integral formation work for as long as you've been involved in Catholic education, though you may not have called it that. Integral formation is a process where we recognize the individual gifts and talents of a student and we seek to develop them to their fullest potential. Integral formation is based upon the deep belief that God created every student with unique and special abilities. It's the awareness that a Catholic school is a place where we value these gifts as part of how God is both revealing Himself in the world and how He is redeeming the world.

So let's make this clear right now. A Catholic school can unashamedly, unequivocally be proud of professional and academic excellence because it is through that excellence that we undertake the tasks of integral formation. Think of it like this: Let's imagine a student we'll call Mary. Mary has been created by God with an amazing talent for languages or math or lacrosse. She may not even know she has this talent when she first comes to your school. However, God already sees a much bigger picture. He knows that if Mary develops this gift, she will grow more fully into the amazing young woman He created her to be. Now, God is not likely to suddenly appear in her bedroom at 2 am in the 8th grade and say in a booming Charlton Heston-style voice, "Mary, Mary... I have created you from all time to play Mozart at Carnegie Hall while simultaneously leading the US Women's Lacrosse Team." Now, let's be clear, God *could* do that if He wanted to. He's God, after all. But, as He may choose not to, how exactly will Mary have *any* chance of discovering these talents, developing them and seeing them flourish at their highest potential?

Imagine a single Catholic teacher. This teacher has a quiet but deep relationship with Jesus. She prays, she reads the New Testament and learns about Jesus more each day. She loves the sacraments and seeks to be open to the movement of grace in her life. She prays, also, for her students every day. One day, this teacher gets a new class. Over the weeks and months she begins to notice that Mary has an interest in music. She provides some encouragement, suggests some books, some famous pieces. Time passes and she remains a constant presence in Mary's journey. Encouraging, teaching, challenging and pushing when needed. While she would never say it out loud, this teacher sees something special in Mary, and she wants this something special to bless Mary, bless the world and to put a smile on God's face. She cares. She knows deep down that this is Mary's gift and that if Mary does not develop it, something will be lost. She also knows that the development of this gift, its perfection, is to the glory of God. Twenty years later the teacher smiles and a slow tear of gratitude rolls down her cheek as she watches Mary take her seat as the principal cellist for the New York Philharmonic.

This is integral formation. It is how we play our part as educators in the full formation of each human person. It is how we partner with God in developing full and authentic human persons. If you're a parent, you intuitively know this is true. Does anything give you more joy than seeing your child find a talent within themselves that makes them and others happy? Does anything give you more joy than seeing them develop that talent to its full potential? So remind yourself of this: these are God's kids you're teaching! How much joy does God experience when you help His kids grow?

Integral formation is the full development of each student in their own capacities and abilities. That is why the mission of forming disciples does not exclude professional excellence as an educator. It does not exclude demanding much of our students and pushing them from time to time. My passionate belief is that our schools must become centers of extraordinary academic excellence, but for the right reasons. Most schools are doing it to avoid losing enrollments, but we can do it because we love young people and want to give God glory.

The Father of Lies

I was not sure when to introduce this, but let's take a moment to talk about evil. Satan is real. Jesus told us that multiple times, so if you don't think Satan exists then either Jesus was wrong or you are. And, while I may not have met you and I am sure you are really smart and all, I'm probably going to place my bets with Jesus on this one. Satan exists. And let's be clear about one thing, Satan has one single plan. Satan understands that he cannot win any ultimate battle with God. The time appointed for his punishment

A Specific View of the Person

In my first book I shared a story about meeting a young woman at a Catholic school.

It was a transformative moment in my life. Theory hit reality with stunning force. I had been speaking about the impact of pornography on young men and women and she came to see me in the break. As she began to cry, she shared how she had been fighting with her parents and had moved in with her boyfriend. He was addicted to hardcore pornography and multiple times a week he forced her into degrading situations that broke her soul. Yes, I reported it to staff and followed up, but so much of the damage had been done.

Why do I share this with you? I share it for the same reason that I talk to teachers in my live seminars about the six million people who died in the holocaust and the roughly 160 million people who died due to the wars unleashed in the 20th century. I spend a lot of time trying to get people to understand that when we see the worst of human behavior, from the sexual trauma of the girl in my seminar to the gulags and gas chambers of the 20th century, we are seeing the same essential problem being enacted over and over again. And what is that problem? Essentially, it's the problem, the sin, of treating a human person in a way that runs contrary to the very deepest truth of what they are.

When we reflect upon the holocaust or the desolate sexual landscape of modern teens, we find, in the ultimate analysis, a horrific and diabolical misreading of the truth of the human person. You can only send someone to the gas chamber if you have no belief in their humanity. You have to see them as less than human.

has been set and it will happen. In light of that, Satan now has only one single option left open. He desires to ensure that as many people as possible are separated from God. He knows his destiny and he wants to ensure that as many people as possible share it with him. His rage is beyond any human conception. He desires only to wound the heart of God and to strike at God's most beloved creation, the human person.

All of this is simply to be very clear that Satan is desperate to stop you uncovering and developing the talents of young people. These talents give glory to God. These talents help young people to find their place in the world. These talents help young people to encounter joy and God and love and purpose and meaning. Satan needs this to stop. As such, you are, in truth, battling a very great enemy, and that's another reason you need to truly cast yourself upon the provision and protection of God.

You need to understand that your role in integral formation is a front-line position in a cosmic battle for the future of each young person. Your encouragement and belief in them is a direct affront to hell and Satan's plan to split each sheep off from the shepherd. So fight back! Be proud of what you do. Take great professional pride in your subject areas and disciplines. Do you see how being a Catholic teacher does not dial down your professionalism and excellence? Instead, it gives it a much deeper nobility, significance and urgency. You can give yourself to becoming the best possible teacher for a reason! You can give your life to uncovering and developing the special talents and abilities of each young person. This is integral formation. Forming each young person into the likeness of Jesus and the fullness of the gifts their Father in heaven willed for them from all eternity. Not a bad way to spend your time! Not bad at all.

A young man can only abuse a teenage girl if he sees her as somehow undeserving of love, respect and care. You have to learn those beliefs. You have to practice them.

As I've already mentioned, my life was changed by the life, thought and writing of Pope John Paul II. As a Polish student attending an underground seminary during Nazi occupation, he saw exactly what happens when enough people misunderstand the truth about the human person. He once wrote that when the wind changed direction the ashes of his countrymen and women would fall on him while he was working in forced labor in a chemical plant. He experienced, personally and viscerally, what happens when people lose site of the truth of the human person.

One of the great things about the study I completed at the Pontifical Institute was that it taught me to think about history, both that of the Church and the wider world in five hundred-year time blocks. In a world obsessed with instant media, it's a good skill to have. The study brought me to see that right at this moment in history, the Catholic Church and – as a result, whether it knows it or not – Catholic education are locked in one great, single struggle. John Paul II understood this with laser-like clarity and spent his entire life, in one way or another, completely focused upon it. And what battle is this? It is the battle over the identity, meaning, value and dignity of the human person.

Does that sound abstract to you? It wasn't abstract for the mothers holding their babies as the Nazis poured pesticide into the injector fans at Auschwitz. It wasn't abstract for the girl in my seminar whose boyfriend was tearing her apart at the deepest level of her being. You see, at the end of the day, what we think a person *is* will determine what we *do*. It is the great towering truth of history. What we think a person is will determine what we do and how we treat them. If you get the truth about the human person wrong, then anything is possible and history proves it over and over again. You have to make a person *subhuman* to be able to dominate and abuse them.

Look at the crises of our time. Endless battles rage over abortion, gender, sex, marriage and euthanasia. All these battles, at their core, are battles about the truth of the person. They are battles over conflicting ideas about what it means to be a person. John Paul commented about the debates over human sexuality like this:

> *"Sexual morality is within the domain of the person. It is impossible to understand anything about it without understanding what the person is, its mode of existence, its functioning, its powers. The personal order is the only proper plane for all debate on matters of sexual morality."*

I love how he states that you cannot understand *anything* about these issues if you do not understand the truth about the person. The truth of the person is the single most crucial battle of our age. So what does it have to do with you and with your place within Catholic education?

The Catholic Church proposes a single great truth about the human person. Importantly, you have to understand that the Church did not invent this truth or come up with it as useful theory to help people get along with each other. The Church received this truth from sacred Scripture. In Genesis, God states with zero ambiguity, "Let us make man in our image and likeness." Before anyone loses their mind over the gender-specific language, *man* in the Hebrew translates as *the human person.* Right at the very beginning of both creation and salvation history, the supreme God, the sole creative force of the entire cosmos, of all that is seen and unseen, makes a decision that humanity will be made in the image and likeness of the eternal Trinity.

At this point I could take a little tour into the sunlit forests of Trinitarian and philosophical anthropology. The views are magnificent and it's worth the trip, but I think if we turn down that road right now we won't make it back before dark. Suffice to say, there is a vast and fascinating body of theology on the manner in which we mirror the image and likeness of God. But for now, let's simply hold on to the fact that every human life is made in the image and likeness of God. Every human life is willed into existence by God. Every human life matters. Every human life is precious. Why? Simple! Because God made them. That's it.

Every human life matters because it matters to God. You know that colleague in your faculty you can't stand? They are made in God's image and have unspeakable value, dignity and worth due to that single fact. You know that student who drives you crazy? They are made in God's image and He loves them. You know that parent who is so in-your-face and unappreciative? They were made in the image of the eternal Trinity and have the most incredible value to God.

Pope Benedict XVI put it like this:

> *"God's love does not distinguish between the infant in the mother's womb or the child or the youth or the adult or the older person. In each one, God sees His image and likeness. Human life is a manifestation of God and His glory..."*

I released a video on YouTube about this, where I made the point that there are zero hierarchies in God's economy, in God's kingdom. As humans we are brilliant at creating all sorts of hierarchies.

We have them for looks, wealth, talent, fame. Remember that time you did not get picked for a team, asked on a date or invited to apply for that big promotion? Well, that's because as humans we have scales and hierarchies and titles, and we apportion human value on all sorts of broken systems and beliefs. God just doesn't do that. In the Old Testament it's almost comical how often God disappointed the Israelites for not being anything like the gods of the pagan nations surrounding them. He was just so different. In fact, the term holiness basically means *otherness*. God is the great other. What He values is so different to what we value at times.

All of this is simply to say that a Catholic school, if it wants to be authentically and genuinely Catholic, *must* be a place where God's vision of the human person is not some vague ideal, but a real and living filter that guides *all* that we do. My experience over the years has been that many schools really try to do this well. And no, I am not ignoring the abuse crisis. Despite the criminal and evil acts perpetrated by a minority and then hidden by wolves masquerading as shepherds, so many Catholic educators really do care about young people and it is to their eternal credit.

A Catholic school is a place where *everything* must be filtered through a very specific view of the human person as made in the image and likeness of God. Every student, colleague, office staff, janitor or parent that is in a Catholic school community is made in the image and likeness of God. And yes, so is everyone outside a Catholic school, but I have to get this book done somehow so I am narrowing my focus.

This view of the preciousness of each person is not only about how we treat each other in a Catholic school, but also about how we educate students about the same ethos. Students *must* leave our Catholic schools with an indelible mark on their consciousness and their intellect that human life is precious. Both Benedict and John Paul were relentless in talking about a culture of death and the dictatorship of relativism. We have to fight back by building a culture of life. I do it by speaking and writing. You need to do it by how you shape, educate and inspire your students to see the value of every human life.

This great quote from the Church documents on education makes it crystal clear:

> *"She establishes her own schools because she considers them as a privileged means of promoting the formation of the whole person, since the school is a center in which a specific concept of the world, of the human person and of history is developed and conveyed."*

Read those words slowly. It talks about a *specific* concept of the human person and history. We are not another option in the supermarket aisle of cultural relativism. We need to stop apologizing and start pushing back while there is still something to defend and to promote. We have a *specific* vision of the human person. We have a *specific* vision of history and of God's action in it. We are going to get nowhere and worse than nowhere if we fear being seen as bigoted for taking a position and communicating it to the students. If a house is on fire, is a firefighter a bigot for presenting his ideas to the people on the second floor?

Let me be really clear. If students leave our schools with no idea about the value and dignity of the human person and why the Catholic Church defends that dignity, then we should hang our heads in shame. We should be, and may well be, eternally embarrassed at our cowardice, laziness and lack of zeal. If God can start his Church with an uneducated fisherman with anger-management issues and a broad yellow stripe down his back, then He can do anything with you and me. We have zero excuse. Our students need our courage and a forthright, living example of what it means to know the value of the person.

It's also crucial that this is not some nice idea to which we give some vague nodding acquiescence. It has to be real. Romans 12:9 makes it clear that our love for others must be sincere. It must be real. The vision of the human person is a lovely idea until some irate parent wants to climb over your desk. Human dignity is a noble cause until that one student treats you with contempt one time too many. Our creation in God's image and likeness is a wonderful thought until one of your colleagues slacks off and leaves you with extra marking or substitute classes. We have to actually live this stuff. We have to pray for the grace and holiness to become living examples of this belief to our students. It's really hard. It can be painful. But so was Calvary.

Later in the book I am going to outline *how* we actually become more capable of living this way, of actually living and witnessing to the truth about the value of every person. But for now, we need to start thinking about it. How are the weakest students treated in your school? How does the principal treat the staff? Who or what is celebrated and valued and why? How are we modeling to students what we actually believe, that each of them is made in God's image?

Three Key Things

So, there are three key things that make up the mission that *is* your Catholic school. Here they are one last time. Try to hold on to these, let them settle into your daily thinking and become a part of how you reflect upon all that you're doing.

1. Catholic schools exist to make disciples. Catholic schools are not an afterthought or something that bishops do for hobbies. They are an extension, a privileged means of what the Catholic Church is doing in history. Your school exists to help young people encounter the real and risen Jesus Christ, to become his life-long disciples, and to find a home in his Church. It's important to recognize, of course, that parents are the primary educators of their own children and the buck of faith formation ultimately stops with them. But let's play our part and create deeply Christ-centered Catholic schools where we help this process take root and grow strong.

2. Catholic schools are deeply committed to integral formation. We are not Catholic madrassas. We can take the both/and approach. We can have both discipleship *and* academic, artistic, sporting, musical excellence. Integral formation is all about recognizing and encouraging and forming the incredible, unique and vibrant gifts inside every single student. As we help each student find and develop their talents, we are directly partnering with God in how He is redeeming the world. Remember also that Satan is incredibly committed to stopping you and making sure every student is cut off from their gifts and from growing closer to God.

3. Catholic schools must be unapologetic for holding a Biblical view of the human person as made in the image and likeness of God. Your school must be a place where every person is treated in a *specific* way because they were created by God. All their value and dignity comes from that truth. Your school needs to be a place where each conversation, lesson, interaction and initiative is filtered through this lens.

So, if this is the mission, why does it seem so hard to attain? Why are schools closing? Why are teachers burning out? Why do students often leave us with so little faith? Well, my friend, I have some good news. I think I know the answer…

You cannot do a supernatural task with natural resources

– Jonathan Doyle

Chapter 3

The Simple Equation

The sound of snoring is never ideal when you're a professional speaker. I've shared the story of our first-ever student seminar, but now let me tell you about my first-ever staff seminar. Ever been in a room where no one wanted to be? I mean apart from your classroom last lesson on a Friday. Imagine the waiting room at the dentist, that kind of thing. We had been asked to come and speak to staff at a Catholic high school. The person who booked us cared about the issues. Karen and I cared about the issues. No one else cared about the issues. Awkward! We walked in. I wanted to walk out. It reminded me of those old western movies where someone walks into the saloon and the piano stops.

We gave it two hundred percent. We joked, we enthused, we avoided annoying activities and death-by-PowerPoint. I think we even brought snacks. Who doesn't like snacks? Short of a full tap-dancing routine and juggling bears, we gave it everything. The piano never started up again. The saloon was closed.

I'm really not making it up, but at one point I was giving it my very best when a lady in the front row, God bless her, fell asleep and started snoring. Ironically, I was discussing sex at that very moment. I took some consolation in the fact that if someone falls asleep when you're talking about sex, they probably have way bigger problems than your seminar can fix.

Cynicism

What I encountered that day, however, became something of a pattern. In every room of Catholic teachers I visited, I began to notice a relatively constant phenomenon. Cynicism. Even when I began to focus less on pastoral and relationship issues of students and talk more about Catholic ethos, identity and teaching itself, the pattern held constant. In any given room I began to encounter several core groups. A majority of people found me unique. The standard of most professional development seminars was so low that as long as you had a pulse people were curious. The fact that I was animated, took a position and delivered it with a lot of energy made me stand out. Kind of like the Liberace of staff professional development without the bling. At the end of each seminar I would then encounter a very small group of deeply devout or committed Catholics. They would sneak up furtively and say things like, "I've been teaching here for thirty years and no one has ever said this stuff... Thank you so much." Then they'd glance around to make sure no one had seen them, and scamper off. But throughout the day, I would encounter a relatively constant stream of cynicism.

I became extremely adept at picking cynicism in all its many hues and colors. There was "the snorter" – they would wait till I made an optimistic or encouraging comment and then snort. There was "the eye-roller" – not quite as vocal as the snorter, but always rolling their eyes just high enough to be sure you saw them. There would also usually be the occasional "scoffer" and a few "whisperers" and the dreaded Kamikaze. The Kamikaze would wait till you said something nice about the sacraments or priests or famous saints, and then they'd dive right on in with an outrageous comment about clerical sexual abuse, female priesthood or some other weird or wacky intrigue from *The Da Vinci Code* or a Vatican Zionist banking scandal straight from the pages of the *National Enquirer*. The Kamikaze ruined your flow. I guess that's what Kamikazes do.

At first I thought that the cynicism I encountered was unique to my country, Australia. Our founding narrative is high on cynicism and suspicion of authority. When a nation is founded by prison inmates, its people tend not to be an optimistic bunch, really. As I began to speak more in the USA, I found a greater optimism and openness embedded in American can-do exceptionalism, but my contacts there assured me that cynicism was an ever-present reality for them as well. So where does this cynicism come from? Why is it a problem? Why should we care?

Supernatural Task, Natural Resources

The actor Jeff Bridges once said that cynics are just crushed romantics. I like that. Every teacher's had a first day in the classroom. Every teacher has, at some point, experienced some excitement, hope or expectation at being a part of the lives of young people. Every teacher, at some point, has held hopes of making a difference. So what happens? There is a paradox here. In some ways, the descent into cynicism can seem complex. It can be stress, burnout, difficult students, difficult colleagues and all the many challenges that make up modern teaching. It's also fair to say that different personality types might be at play. Do extroverts survive longer in teaching while introverts crumble under the burden of human interaction, noise and busyness? Perhaps. But I want to suggest that the cause of this cynicism that plagues Catholic schools can also be very simple, and it will be the central theme of this entire book.

Before laying out my thesis I want to make the point that cynicism does not have to be the go-to experience the longer you stay in the vocation of Catholic education. It's not some kind of inexorable Star Trek-style tractor beam dragging you endlessly toward shortness of temper, early retirement and a strange twitch when young people walk past. Is it possible to not only survive the vocation of being a Catholic teacher, but to actually thrive? I believe it is. In fact, I've committed much of my professional life to the idea that it is. I hope I can prove that to you in the pages that follow. I believe that if you're reading this, it's highly likely that you do have a vocation. It's highly likely that God called you into this vocation to help bring about His kingdom purposes. You were created with the ability to not only do this, but to do it very well and to find joy and purpose and fulfillment in it. And if that's true, then it's not your task to survive teaching – it's God's job to sustain you.

My central premise is that what is happening in Catholic education is simply this: *vast numbers of good people are wiping themselves out trying to do a supernatural task with only natural resources.* There you have it. I pray you will keep reading because I want to flesh this out for you. I want to give you some insights and tools that will truly help you thrive. I want you to be a blessing to your students, but also to your family and those who don't want to live with a cranky, exhausted, cynical bear with a sore head.

Cynicism is essentially the end result of trying to do a supernatural task with only natural resources. Cynicism is what happens when you get tired. Cynicism is what happens when you've given it all by

Tuesday and Friday is beyond your capacity. It's like the old saying about personal budgets that there is always too much "month" left at the end of the money. We just can't give any more. There is nothing left. Rather than admit our weakness, uncertainty and dependence, we shift into survival mode by blaming the environment, the system, the principal, the bishop, the Pope, the parents, the internet. We blame anything that will hide the truth that we are just tired and worn out and we can't easily go on.

The problem with cynics is that they don't actually go far enough. They experience the frustration, the tiredness, the let-downs and they assume it's a problem in the system. *"If only there was more time, more money, better behaved kids, then I would be happier."* Once you ransom your happiness to the behavior of other people and complex systems, you're in big trouble. The truth about the crisis in Catholic education, teacher retention and burnout is simply that we all thought it was a case of tweaking the system or maybe trying harder or getting more funds. It's not. The real problem is that most of us have forgotten that the *vocation* of Catholic education is a supernatural task. When you try to do something supernatural using finite human resources, then it's a recipe for slow, barely perceptible but unequivocal, eventual failure.

Imagine having an incurable disease but suddenly a doctor walks in and tells you they have found a miracle cure. All you have to do is receive it. My message about Catholic education is a little similar. There is a way out. There is a way out of cynicism and burnout and school closures, and it does not really depend that much on you. In fact, pretty much everything wonderful ever achieved by men and women in the Catholic Church happened when those same men and women realized the one big secret I am trying to let you in on. You see, it's not about you really. It's not about your finite, limited human capacity and all your frailties and failings.

There is a much bigger story coming. What story is that? It's the story of what happens when an infinite God, the same God who sustains the entire cosmos, is given access to your life in a new and deeper way. I mean, seriously, look at St. Francis. The guy was, like, five foot nothing and ran around naked for a while and yet he essentially changed the entire Church, much of Western culture and his impact is still felt centuries later. How long do you really want to play the game of trying to do this supernatural task with your limited resources?

Increasing Expectations, Finite Time

I was the first student at my school not to do math in my senior year. I think a few of the staff got together and said, "Do we really want the hassle?" I had been kicked out of my previous class – Miss Rassmuss's 11th grade remedial math class – for yelling out loud, "Come on, Miss, you need to stop Harrassmussing me!" I thought it was a moment of comedic genius. The play on her surname, the perfect execution, the adoring crowd. Sadly, her capacity to appreciate intellectual humor was rather unrefined. She sent me on the walk of shame, never to return. It's a pity because I really liked quadratic equations. I could stare at them for hours.

All this is by way of highlighting the truth that while I can turn a phrase or type out a few words, times tables are about the extent of my mathematical achievements. However, I want to share with you one formula I think you will be familiar with. I call it the *simple equation*. The simple equation is the truth that the education profession is experiencing a particular trend at this moment in history. Government expectations on teachers are increasing. Parental expectations on teachers are increasing. Student expectations on teachers are increasing. In an aspirational and utilitarian culture, teachers are increasingly being seen as *service providers.* They are there to perform a function, which is to increase college and university entrance scores.

In practice, it goes like this. A university academic or politician releases a white paper or calls a press conference. They make dire predictions about the state of literacy or numeracy or the nation's ranking on some global educational attainment table. Next day this appears with a lurid headline in national papers. Social media and talkback radio light up and eventually teachers are held responsible.

So, in essence, the simple equation is just this: *increasing expectations in an environment of finite time*. Do more with less. Do more with no time for reflection. Do more with no time for creativity, reading or rest. Do more. Do more. Do more. More administration. More feedback, please. More individually tailored learning plans for diverse learning styles. More faculty meetings, more parent conferences, more student interventions. All in an environment of finite human time and energy. All this in an environment of increasingly complex student mental health and pastoral care scenarios. This is the core of the crisis. Do more, more, more in a more and more challenging environment.

"Apart from me you can do nothing."

John 15:5

Chapter 4

Tools and Fuels

I'm a kind of "death before dishonor" guy. For most of my life I have taken exercise really seriously. I know how to suffer. In fact, to be honest, I like it. My grandfather died at the age of forty-four of a heart attack, and my father spent most of his life out of shape. I was not keen to follow the family path. So, for me, stopping while training or racing is unthinkable. It's something I had never done until one fateful morning.

Fitz's Hill is hidden in the rolling hills south of Australia's capital city, Canberra. It's only a short ride from my home and a place I know well. After twenty years as a runner, I had finally discovered the sublime beauty of expensive road bikes and the supportive embrace of lycra. Cycling became a very great passion, and Fitz's Hill is well known by the local cycling community. In fact, it has shaped more than a few local legends who have gone on to win on the world stage.

Each year there is a special event called the Fitz's Challenge. You can take your pain in a 40 mile version, a 100 mile version or the epic 165 mile version. The "challenge" part is not so much in the distance as it is in the fact that the longer version takes in three major climbs, the steepest of which is Fitz's Hill. It's long, it's brutally steep and it has a few false crests and bends that convince you that you've almost made the summit. You haven't.

And so I began. I woke at about 4 am, so excited to be having a crack at a big event like this. A friend picked me up and we drove in the pre-dawn darkness to the marshaling area. And off we went. The first 37 miles were fine. I rode at the front of the lead group and felt good. I was fit, experienced and knew the course reasonably well.

Earlier that morning I had taken time to prepare two bottles of a special electrolyte and carbohydrate solution. I figured it'd be a long day and I was going to need supplements to get me through. My jersey pockets were also filled with special carbohydrate gel sachets and bars. I was set. The morning was relatively warm, so on those first 37 miles I drank freely from the pre-prepared bottles with little clue about what was about to unfold.

I made it through the first couple of hours and soon enough found myself at the base of Fitz's Hill. You know how those guys in the Tour de France who win the mountain stages are so lean? You know how they weigh about 120 pounds and soar up those lofty peaks like nimble gazelles? Yeah? Well...I'm not like that. Don't get me wrong. I'm fit and lean and, to blow my own trumpet, probably fitter than about ninety-five percent of guys my age. But climbing? Umm...not exactly the nimblest of gazelles.

As I pushed onto the lower slopes of Fitz's Hill, I quickly encountered my first major problem. Guys far less fit than I am seemed to be passing me. Now, if I were holy I would have thought nothing much about it. However, God still has a long way to go working on my competitive streak. The blows to my cycling ego were worse than the growing pain in my legs. Why were these guys climbing faster? Well, imagine driving a manual car up a mountain but you suddenly discover you only have one gear. Other cars surge past you working through the gearbox with ease, but you're going nowhere fast. I discovered to my later embarrassment that I had thought nothing about the gearing ratio on my bike. I was essentially climbing Everest with a Sherpa, two llamas and half of Kathmandu strapped to my back. I was going nowhere.

I am fighting with everything in me right now to stop these next few paragraphs turning into a rich and lyrical exploration of the glorious science of bike maintenance and gear ratios. For you, I will control myself. Suffice to say, I had the wrong gear setup on the bike. I was riding with a standard racing drive-train instead of a dedicated climbing rig. Put simply, when you know you're going into mountain-goat territory, you need to change your gears. I was about to discover new vistas of pain and failure.

Yet on I pressed. The utter ignominy, the social death, the self-recrimination of each moment was omnipresent. I struggled on. How can I describe this? Imagine trying to cycle up a massive hill but some big guy is pulling you backward on each pedal stroke. And the great revelation was this: for the task at hand I had the wrong tools. The situation called for a particular response in advance, but I had not made it. I could not effectively do the task with the tools I had. The minutes passed slowly. The pain increased. The summit eventually rolled beneath me. I drank the rest of my fluids and rolled down the other side as close to a near-death experience as I have ever known.

Shortly thereafter I was attacked by one of our local bird species, obviously annoyed at my gear selection as well. I was tired, feeling unwell, but extremely hungry and desperate to reach the turn-around marker and food stop.

When I reached the food stop I was a mess. I was also beyond caring, so I ate the food, all of it. I ate pretty much everything I could see, most of which had a sugar content to rival the annual sugar production of a small Caribbean nation. I ate and I ate and I ate. Oh, how sweet is hindsight. I climbed on the bike and dragged myself up the first hill of the return leg like a Minke whale beaching on a sugar encrusted beach.

With two major climbs and about 60 miles still to go, I knew I was in trouble. I felt very strange and incredibly sick. I wanted to lie down and groan. I decided to keep pedaling and groan. Same groaning, just more forward momentum. At the base of the first remaining climb, I finally rolled to a stop. I had never stopped on any race or ride in my life. I knew that I could somehow make it up this next hill. I understood that if I could do that then I could probably roll back down. But I also knew that would still leave one more climb and another 25 miles of climbing to the final finish line. I stopped and summoned every ounce of commitment and strength I had ever possessed, and I did what any man would do in my situation: I gave up and called Karen to come pick me up.

Breaking It Down

In the weeks that followed, I pondered. I mused. I read and discussed and I forensically dissected my inglorious and epic failure. It came down to two things. First, I had the wrong equipment. Second, I had a terrible hydration and eating plan. One of the things that sugar does is impact how your stomach actually empties itself. It can retard the effectiveness by which fluid and food leave the stomach and are converted by the body into available energy. Interestingly, under the conditions I was racing the body can often burn up to 750 calories per hour, but can only replace about 350 from any source. Too much sugar can also irritate the stomach lining under race conditions. All this is a fancy way of saying that I made myself sick. Instead of drinking mostly water with the option of some electrolytes, if needed later, I had dumped the wrong fuels into my system from the get-go. I was literally making myself sick. Combined with the wrong gear ratios, I had set myself up for massive failure. It all came down to what I started calling the wrong *tools* (gears) and the wrong *fuels*. I walked away and realized that in sport and, as I want to argue, in life, if you attempt anything worthwhile with the wrong tools and the wrong fuels, then you are in for trouble.

Two weeks later I flew to that little island you can see off the bottom of Australia called Tasmania. I did a 150 mile race up bigger hills. I drank water. I ate carefully. I changed my gears. I finished in record time, feeling great. I had learned the hard lesson of the wrong tools and the wrong fuels.

Months later, I was invited to speak to five hundred teachers in Florida. I'm a big believer that one of the most important things to do in a good speech or a decent book is to offer people some stories or metaphors that they can hang on to after you've gone.

It was here that the tools and fuels metaphor began to take shape. As I reflected upon the mission failures that appeared to be increasingly common for so many Catholic schools and dioceses, I felt a certain resonance with the experience I'd had on the bike that dark day. I began to wonder if some of what we were seeing was a case of either the wrong approach (tools) or the wrong energy source (fuels). Why were so many teachers burning out? Why was there so much cynicism? Why were no disciples being made? Could we be using the wrong tools and the wrong fuels?

The Wrong Tools?

This won't take long. I don't think we have a problem with tools. By this I mean that you only have to spend about five minutes on my social media feeds to see how many teachers in Catholic schools are deeply interested in pedagogy. Honestly, I have no idea what most of them are talking about, but it does sound rather exciting! All sorts of acronyms and metaphors and clever ideas about learning styles and critical thinking abound. I make the point in my seminars that I just don't think that we are going to solve the great issues of Catholic education with better pedagogy. That does not mean that pedagogy is unimportant. It is very important. It's just not at the core of the real issues we are facing.

I concede that we can always look for new and better ways to communicate the truths of faith. There are always new ways to help young people experience the reality of Jesus's presence and we need to keep pursuing those methodologies. In fact, one of the great things about Catholic education *is* professionalism. When you understand that your work is an offering to God and a key part of how He is redeeming the world, then being professional is a magnificent way to give glory to God, serve young people, fulfill your potential and serve the world. Not a bad way to live.

My point, however, is that these methodologies and pedagogies are available already. You can find them, study them, implement them. And, if they work, you should. But if our challenges in Catholic schools were simply about pedagogy or what I'm calling *tools*, then I think we would have worked it out by now. So where does that leave us?

The Wrong Fuels?

The fact is that on that long day on the bike I probably could have coped with the gear problem, the tools problem. It would have been far easier with the right equipment, no doubt, but I still could have got it done. What actually finished me was one hundred percent the wrong fuels. With the wrong fuels I simply had no chance. I was sick and getting worse by the minute. I simply could no longer do what I had come to do. My mission had become unattainable.

As time passed, I began to apply the fuels metaphor to what I was seeing in Catholic education. Why were we not really reaching kids? Why were so many teachers leaving? Why were many of those who stayed so cynical? Why were many schools no longer vibrant or hope-filled or optimistic about creating disciples, integral formation or helping each student develop an authentic view of the human person? Could it be possible that what I was seeing was in fact the result of individual teachers, schools and entire dioceses making one great mistake?

I began to think. If Jesus established a Church and He promised to never abandon or leave that Church, and that Church established schools, then why were these schools failing? If Jesus was able to sustain the entire universe, surely sustaining Catholic schools would be a walk in the park? I began to think that there was no way that the problem could be with Jesus. It had to be with us. There was something we were doing, or *not* doing, that was causing the mission failure. Scripture and tradition were clear that Jesus was faithful. He promised to not leave us as orphans. As well as telling us to make disciples at the ascension, He had already promised us that after He ascended the Holy Spirit would be sent to us. There was no way he would break that promise. Again, the problem could not be with Jesus. It had to be with us.

And so I realized that we were all making one fundamental mistake. It was so simple but so widespread. It was so obvious upon reflection, but so hard to notice in the moment. And what was that mistake? What is the one great mistake that all my travel and speaking and writing and thinking and praying have led me to? Simply this: *you cannot do a supernatural task with only natural resources!* In other words, you will never succeed at the mission of Catholic education without the one source of energy that is utterly crucial.

From Florida to LA, from London to Sydney, I have been making the same point over and over and over again. What is the cause of burnout? It's trying to do a supernatural task with only natural resources. Why don't we make disciples? Because we keep trying to do a supernatural task with only natural resources. Why are we not truly effective in the area of integral formation? Because we keep trying to do a supernatural task with only natural resources.

Back to Our Mission

I've said this before but it's worth repeating, Catholic education is not like any other educational endeavor. It is not about imparting facts or improving critical thinking or developing 21st-century learners. Those things can all happen, and should happen, in a Catholic school, but they are not the reason our schools were established. They are a by-product of something else. A Catholic school is a *spiritual* place. It begins with a very specific view of the human person, of their creation in the image and likeness of God. It begins with a specific vision of each person's eternal destiny and the incredible possibility of their lives. We also know that Satan is utterly committed to ensuring no young person meets Jesus or loves the Church. That's important because it means your school is a place of spiritual battle. It's a place where good and evil wrestle for the heart and mind and spirit of every student.

A Catholic school is a unique place. You must understand that. It has a deeply spiritual meaning and purpose, and to operate as if it didn't is extremely problematic and explains so much of our current problem. My central thesis is that the *only* way we can save Catholic education, the only way we can achieve its mission, is nothing short of a radical dependence on the person of Jesus Christ and His power.

All the great figures of Christian history *always* ended up with this single realization. Think of St. Paul, who wrote that he looked upon everything that had ever seemed important to him and realized it was like garbage and refuse compared to the supreme advantage of knowing Jesus. Think of Aquinas, writing what is probably the most voluminous human exposition of all theology, his Summa. Upon completion he said, "All that I have written is but chaff." He knew that all his human wisdom was nothing compared to the reality of God's nature, His power and His purposes.

I am calling for a radical return. I am calling for us all to wake up to the futility of our human striving and sophistry and return to a deep dependence on the person of Jesus Christ and His plan and purpose for our schools. Anything less than this is foolishness. We've been trying to do this on our own for so long. It's not working.

The Simple Equation (Once Again)

The American pastor Loren Sandford once said that there are two ways in life to learn. You can learn with a gentle word or from a piece of timber over the head. I always liked that. His years of ministry had taught him that people will either learn from a quiet word in their ear about what is happening or they will have to be hit over the head by the metaphorical lump of wood we call life. In short, you can learn easy or you can learn hard.

Here is what is about to happen in the education space over the next decades. I'll tell you and then you can decide what you want to do.

1. There will be more parental expectation as parents become increasingly aspirational and expect their children to do well.
2. There will be more expectation from students because they will sense the pressure coming from their own parents. In the developed world students are already suing schools and teachers if they don't get into the colleges and universities they want.
3. Students' mental health and pastoral issues will become more complex. Schools and teachers will be expected to deal with these issues.
4. Government will place more and more pressure on schools for outcomes.
5. Schools will be increasingly expected by government to provide life skills and other programs outside their normal curricula.
6. Technology will add (not remove) complexity.
7. Administrative and feedback tasks will increase.
8. Time and energy will remain finite.

Please read point number 8 really carefully again. *Time and energy will remain finite.* Points 1 to 7 are just my random musings. You could add many more and you know I am right. Look again at point number 8 – *time and energy will remain finite.*

As I explained in Chapter 3, this is what I have been calling the *simple equation.* Demands are increasing while your time and energy are remaining finite. In fact, your energy may be going backward. As you know, math was never my gig, but even I can figure out what this means. What happens when you stretch a rubber band tighter and tighter? What happens when you keep adding demands and not increasing supply? Something. . .eventually. . .breaks! And that something is not just the system...it's the teacher as well.

In my seminars I make the point that if you come from a great family, had a nice childhood and have a personal psychology, you will most likely buck the trend. You may survive for many years. We all know one or two teachers who go the distance. But my reply to that would be to ask, how much more might they have achieved if they deployed the solution I am going to offer in the pages that follow? The fact is that many teachers are struggling and many are tired. We need to do something. It's also worth pointing out that so many times, both in Scripture and in history, the people who accomplished so much for the kingdom of God were rarely the ones with perfect backgrounds and a great personal psychology. They were often the ones who had run down so many blind alleys that they finally stopped running and allowed themselves to be caught by grace.

Apart from Him, You Can Do Nothing

I don't want to ever be accused of not doing enough to try and get people's attention on this topic. However, if you disagree with my premise, I am going to go over your head and appeal to someone you just can't really argue with: Jesus.

I've always loved the farewell discourses in John's Gospel. I love their poignant tone. There is such an authentic intimacy there. In chapter 15, Jesus says something that every Catholic teacher needs to deeply internalize:

> *"I am the vine; you are the branches. If you remain in me and I in you, you will bear much fruit; apart from me you can do nothing. If you do not remain in me, you are like a branch that is thrown away and withers; such branches are picked up, thrown into the fire and burned."*

Apart from me you can do nothing. If I could just get every Catholic teacher in the world to deeply think about those words. *Apart from me you can do nothing.* Notice that Jesus does not say, "Apart from me you will be less effective." Notice he does not say, "Apart from me you will do some okay things, but with me you could do even more." He makes it incredibly clear that apart from Him we can do *nothing.* Interestingly, given how much I have talked about burnout, Jesus even makes the point that disciples of His who do not stay connected to Him end up, metaphorically at least, being burned. Apart from Jesus, we wither and die. Apart from Jesus, we are ineffective. Apart from Jesus, we are burned up by the demands and pressures of life. How much clearer can it be? Obviously not clear enough or we would all have figured it out by now.

My premise is that a radical return by Catholic educators to both relationship *with* and dependence *upon* Jesus is the only fuel that will sustain us to fulfill our mission. It is the only fuel that will allow us to overcome the inexorable pull of the simple equation of increasing demands and finite resources. If he can sustain the universe, He can sustain you. And not only sustain you, but empower and anoint you to do things you have not even imagined yet. I believe this with all my soul. It's my life's work. My task is simply to tell you that without Him you are either going to burn out and eventually quit and walk away or be incalculably less effective than you otherwise could have been.

I have another favorite saying, 'There is no point climbing the ladder of success if the ladder is up against the wrong wall.' In a similar way, there is no point having the world's greatest lesson plans and getting promoted and applauded if God had other plans for you and for your impact upon your students. Our task is to know Him and become the teacher or leader that He knows we can become *in* Him. You only get one life. Do you really want to take the risk? Do you really think you are just going to outwork, out-plan, or outrun the pressures that are coming down the line?

I am not referring to maybe having some nice thoughts about Jesus. I am not suggesting you might pray for five minutes a day. I am suggesting that you re-orient your entire life to a complete dependence upon Him and His saving power in your life. I am suggesting you give up your own feeble attempts to make your life and career work and fall into the arms of the Holy Spirit and His counsel and direction. I am suggesting that you surrender your vocation and each moment to the One who is able to do exceedingly, abundantly and beyond all that you could hope or imagine.

As well as the vine and branches metaphor, we also have the incredible quote from St. Paul in Philippians 4:13: "I can do all things through Christ who strengthens me." Keep in mind that Paul, like so many of the great Biblical figures, had to be confronted with his own incapacity. So many times God had to break His chosen vessels. So many times, He had to find ways to make people realize that their own limited ability was never going to be enough of a platform for Him to carry out His plans and purposes. Paul came to learn that all his reliance on his ethnic, sectarian and personal credentials was utterly meaningless to God and to what God wanted to accomplish through Paul's life. He had to learn that it was through radical dependence upon Christ that he was to accomplish so much and change the very face of human history.

Are you getting this? Is it penetrating your own self-reliance and all the schemes and plans and coping strategies that have brought you this far in life? You can choose one of two possible options. The first is the path of limited effectiveness at best and burnout at worse. The second is what Richard Rohr calls the "path of descent." This is the path into a kind of personal death, the death of your own reliance and trust in your own cleverness and ability. On the other side of that death is the resurrection. It's a new life, where the same power that raised Christ Jesus from the dead works through your own vocation and life and body and hands and words and lesson plans and conversations and interactions.

So, let's turn our attention to how we are going to do this.

"...all the faithful of Christ of whatever rank or status, are called to the fullness of the Christian life and to the perfection of charity."

Lumen gentium

Chapter 5

Becoming a Saint

Some things in the spiritual life are so darn paradoxical. Life comes through death. We gain everything by letting go of everything. You know the story. Communicating these paradoxes and some of the towering truths of faith, as a speaker, can be enormously difficult. There have been many moments over the years when I have wanted an audience to understand something of great importance. At that moment I want choirs of angels to appear. Trumpets! Fanfare! I want whatever it takes to get people to really understand the magnitude of whatever I am about to say.

That may sound comical or flippant, but I'm actually serious. There really are moments when what I am about to share really matters. And right now is also one of those moments. What I am about to tell you may well be the most important thing as a Catholic that you will hear in this life. If you understand what I am going to tell you and begin to seriously try to live it, then it has the capacity to change your life. In fact, that is the exact purpose of it.

All that's required for you to complete the mission of Catholic education, avoid burnout and change the world is this: *you need to become a saint.* (And this is the moment in which angels are supposed to sigh, and wherever you're sitting right now the clouds should part and a beam of sunlight should fall upon the page and convince you of the veracity of what I'm saying.) All that Catholic education needs is saints. That's it. If St. Francis could alter world history just by becoming a saint, then what's your excuse? At least you're fully dressed.

The Association Subroutine

Now, we have some work to do because a large part of your brain just went on vacation. A large part of your brain just checked out because the moment you heard me tell you that are meant to be a saint your brain began running what I call the *association subroutine.* The association subroutine is like a piece of software that your brain runs whenever it is trying to place an idea into some kind of meaning or context. Associations are simply ways in which we give meaning, context or background to a word. For example, when I say something like "dentist's waiting room" and "root canal," your brain throws up some associations. It associates those words with your life experience and then gives you a framework for what those words mean and what relevance they have for you. It's that old Freudian free-association thing, where the guy with the nicely trimmed goatee pulls words out of a hat and then explains, based upon your response, why your father's choice of aftershave when you were three means you now avoid conflict or have too many cats.

Associations are useful. They allow us to navigate the world more efficiently because we can associate new things to old things. We can project into the future based on what we know about something from the past. And herein lies our great problem. The word "saint" has so many associations for most of us, and most of them are not particularly helpful. Over the years sharing this concept with audiences, we've talked about some of the associations that people call to mind. For many, it's ideas about stained glass windows, excessive piety, being "otherworldly" and abnormal. And there is a rejection of the body and of sexuality. This, of course, is the old gnostic heresy of "spirit good, body bad," which the Church has been trying to kill for the last two thousand years with varying degrees of success.

However people associate the word saint, they rarely, if ever, see it as something even remotely likely to have relevance for their life. I joke with them about the idea that God has some kind of saint factory in heaven and they roll off a conveyor belt and arrive in cribs with their little cherubic hands clasped in prayer. Oh, paahleease...spare me! Even the most cursory reading of Christian history shows that saints come from the most wildly diverse backgrounds. St. Augustine was a drunkard and fornicator who fathered an illegitimate child. St. Ignatius was a soldier at a time in history when warfare was unspeakably barbarous and Geneva was still a small town, yet to give us any sort of convention on the rules of war. And let's not forget St. Mary of Egypt and St. Pelagia the Harlot, who were seasoned operators in the world's oldest profession before they encountered Jesus. Sure, there are plenty of saints who came from pretty pious backgrounds, but there are just as many who didn't. Saints are not made in a factory. They are of the earth. They are of the blood and dust and tears and laughter of the human condition. Only one thing sets them apart. They fell in love with something so far beyond their comprehension that it utterly redirected their lives.

The Real You

Before I try to convince you as to why God plans for you to be a saint, we need to learn a few things about them. One of the best things about becoming a saint is that you get to become fully who you are. Most of our lives, to varying degrees, we've been role-playing. We evolved to place extreme value on social belonging and cohesion. In terms of evolutionary psychology, our brains are highly adapted to fear rejection and being ostracized. Why? Simply because for most of human history if you were rejected by your tribe, clan or village, you died. You starved or got killed by another clan who saw you walking around without your group, or you got eaten by a bear or maybe a lion or a really angry otter. You get the picture – you either starved, got killed or got eaten if your group cut you off. As such, we evolved to read facial gestures, voice tone and hierarchies to ensure our own survival and group flourishing. The downside is that we also learned to accommodate, deny our own identity and kill off our inner self at the same time.

Why does this matter? Because becoming a saint means that all of a sudden our deepest identity is now rooted deeply in God. Saints, while they can be good communicators and diplomats, begin to lose interest in what others really think about them. They only care what God thinks about them and that makes them authentic. Even a basic reading of the Gospels makes it extremely obvious that Jesus had zero interest in what anyone thought of Him.

This means that becoming a saint allows you to come home to your most authentic self. It allows you to stop hiding, game playing and appeasing, and just come home to yourself. God can't use you fully in this life while you're busy being someone else. So the first compelling reason to become a saint is that, maybe for the first time in your life, you can finally become the real you.

A Divine Encounter

The second thing about saints is something I alluded to above. They fall in love. It can be the childlike beauty of how St. Therese of Lisieux related to God, or the more masculine, soldierly way in which St. Ignatius encountered God. Once again, notice how becoming a saint did not obliterate their natural inclinations. Ignatius did not become all flowery and Therese was no Joan of Arc. God seems to simply desire that His saints express His glory by being most fully who they were created to be. How could you not find this compelling for your own life? But for now, back to the love thing. Saints all seem to have had some sort of genuine encounter with the divine. They seem to encounter God and become so taken by Him that the axis of their life shifts in the most remarkable and often dramatic ways. The rest of their life is simply spent living out of the depth of that encounter and ongoing reality.

Saints also become like God. They want what God wants. They begin to see reality the way God sees reality. When you look at Mother Teresa of Calcutta, you are not seeing just a *nice* person. There are lots of nice people in the world, but only one Teresa of Calcutta. Why? She simply began to live her life seeing reality as God saw reality. She began to feel for the sick and dying what God feels for the sick and dying. Her heart began to beat in time with God's. She became like God inasmuch as it was possible for her in this life.

No Hierarchy

The great heresy under which most of us continue to live is that saints are these remarkable otherworldly beings who are handpicked by God like some sort of cosmic Navy Seals. It's just plain not true. They are no different to you and I. They just made a different response and the gates of grace were thrown wide, flooding their souls and changing the world. So let's deal with this heresy quickly.

One of the points I make in my seminars is that before the Second Vatican Council, most of the laity lived under a vague clericalist hierarchy. Priests and bishops were holy and better than others. Nuns were a little further down, but still holy. And then there were the rest of us. Depending on how much Calvinism permeated your theology, we were at best redeemed sinners and at worst depraved and godless worms only a breath away from teetering over the brink of the abyss into unquenchable fire.

My grandfather owned the construction company that rebuilt Liverpool Cathedral after World War II. I have seen old movie footage of the opening, where you see these hierarchies all played out in processions of frocked monsignors and the lay folk kept back behind the barriers. Now, don't get me wrong. I deeply value the priesthood. I am a son of the Church, and all that she holds to be true and teaches I hold to be true also. What I'm getting at is the constant human tendency to split us up into groups of holy and "a-little-less-holy." This is what Jesus was always going after with the Pharisees. He was sick and tired of the idea that if you scrubbed your copper pots while standing on one leg, facing north and wearing the latest phylactery, you were somehow in better standing with God. What Vatican II did, among other things, was present a wonderful new dispensation – the universal call to holiness.

Hidden in a Vatican II document called *Lumen gentium* was the statement:

> *"...all the faithful of Christ of whatever rank or status, are called to the fullness of the Christian life and to the perfection of charity."*

Years later, Pope Benedict provided some more exposition of what this meant:

"What does it mean to be holy? Who is called to be holy? We are often led to think that holiness is a goal reserved for a few elect. St. Paul, instead, speaks of God's great plan and says: 'even as he (God) chose us in him (Christ) before the foundation of the world, that we should be holy and blameless before him' (Ephesians 1:4). And he was speaking about all of us.

"The Second Vatican Council, in the Dogmatic Constitution on the Church, speaks with clarity of the universal call to holiness, saying that no one is excluded: 'The forms and tasks of life are many but holiness is one.'"

There is so much in this. In just a few short lines, centuries of clericalism fall away with the simple reminder that every single one of us is called to holiness. All are called to be saints. Look again at those words from *Lumen gentium*: *"...all the faithful of Christ of whatever rank or status, are called to the fullness of the Christian life and to the perfection of charity."*

No matter what your rank or status. You might be the principal or the janitor, it's irrelevant. What matters is that you are called to the fullness of Christian life. You are called to become fully who you are in Christ. You are called to become authentically yourself so you can become like the God who created you in His own image and likeness. I love how Benedict makes it clear that *"the forms and tasks of life are many but holiness is one."* That means that a janitor can truly become a saint and so can the principal and everyone in between. This is such good news.

A Call to Holiness

The reason I am sharing this is that we have to wake up and take this call to holiness, to sainthood, seriously. How can Catholic educators avoid burnout and cynicism? By becoming saints. How can Catholic teachers make disciples? By becoming saints. How can Catholic teachers create the conditions for integral formation? By becoming saints. How can Catholic teachers help students understand the truth and dignity of the human person? By becoming saints.

There is only one reason that Catholic schools are not achieving their mission. It's simply because we don't have enough saints. And we don't have enough saints because, once again, we're trying to do a supernatural task with natural resources. We lack the right fuels. As a result, there is only one reason that teachers burn out and leave the profession. It's because no one helped them to become saints. The saints started vast initiatives and undertook immense programs but they didn't burn out or quit. Why? Because they were carried by a power vastly beyond themselves. How long are we going to continue this madness? We have to become saints. We have to crave holiness like oxygen. Holiness and not false piety. Real holiness, which is nothing other than desiring to know Jesus, wanting what He wants and being like Him. To see the world like Him and to feel for the world and the broken and the lost what He feels for the world, the broken and the lost. If more funds and clever programs and better classroom management were going to save us, then they would have done so by now. We are like tired, hungry children who kick against the parent who wants to sweep us up and carry us. We have to stop. We have to turn and cast ourselves into the abyss of His presence and be caught and carried by the arms of grace. We will never be the teachers we can be without this. We will never build the schools we need without this. We will never halt the culture of death until we become saints.

The Curious Case of Solanus Casey

At this point in my seminars there is usually some type of stunned silence. People have usually overcome their initial resistance to the idea of sainthood as I seek to break down the associations. However, most still carry a deep conviction that while sainthood matters, it's still for other people. That's when I start to talk about Solanus.

Solanus Casey, known to his family as Barney, was born in September 1870 in Michigan. He was the sixth of sixteen children. He contracted diphtheria as a child, which permanently damaged his voice leaving it impaired and raspy. He had minimal schooling due to farm work, and eventually took various laboring jobs and ended up as a prison guard. One night he witnessed a murder as a sailor stabbed a woman to death in front of him. Deeply shaken, he re-evaluated his life and decided to enter the local diocesan seminary.

His almost non-existent education meant that he struggled massively with the Latin and German texts and simply could not complete the academic formation. He was quietly invited to leave with the suggestion that he maybe consider one of the religious orders. The suggestion was that due to his limited intellect he could become a "simplex" priest, meaning he could say private masses but wouldn't be allowed to preach or hear confessions.

In 1897 he joined the Franciscan seminary in Detroit and managed to limp through the formation process. He was given a number of short-term placements, but there was a strong sense that nobody knew what to do with this shy, uninspiring friar. Finally, in 1924, he was sent to work at the St. Bonaventure Convent in Detroit, where he would spend the next twenty-one years.

For all of those twenty-one years, Solanus Casey pretty much had one job. He was to sit in a small room and open the door when visitors rang the bell. He would then carry their bags or sit and talk to them while more "important" people were summoned to deal with more important matters. Solanus just kept opening the door. For twenty-one years he opened the door, sat with people and listened to them. And then something began to happen.

Visitors began to notice that this quiet, almost awkward priest had an unusual ability to provide profound spiritual counsel and that he was possessed of the most extraordinary compassion. He began to pray for people to be healed and they were healed. He began to have spiritual and supernatural insight into people's problems and pains, which they had never shared with another soul. Each Wednesday he was allowed to say one Mass, and more and more people began to come to experience his compassion, gentleness and healing. But whenever he wasn't praying in silence before the Eucharist in the chapel, he was just opening doors, carrying bags and listening to people.

After his death in 1957, a cause for his canonization commenced. In 1995 he was declared Venerable Solanus Casey. He is on track to being recognized as a saint because he opened a door with love. There is much to this. First, a small technical detail I've always enjoyed sharing. The Catholic Church does not *make* saints. She simply *recognizes* them. That's an important distinction.

God makes saints, the Church simply draws them to our attention so we can look at their lives and see what happens when grace builds upon nature.

I want you to deeply integrate the message of Solanus Casey for your life. He became a saint by simply loving God and others *exactly* where he was planted. He did not start an order or rebuild the Church. He just opened a door. For twenty-one years, he just opened a door. God led him to holiness right in the middle of his vocation. Notice how God, once again, uses the humble and small to subvert our ideas about holiness, usefulness and sainthood. Solanus failed the seminary. He had no wonderful gifts of oratory or a brilliant intellect. In fact, he basically lost his voice as a child. But did you notice how God *spoke* through Solanus anyway?

Blooming Where You're Planted

What I need you to understand is that if God can make a saint of an illiterate farm worker from Michigan who could barely speak, then what is stopping us? What reason can you give to yourself, to God, to anyone else, to suggest that you cannot become a saint in the very location God has planted you right now? Perhaps you may never be officially *recognized* by the Catholic Church, but that is ultimately irrelevant. The goal of holiness, the goal of sainthood is not recognition. The goal of sainthood is love, and love is God and God is love and it's the path to authenticity and happiness and finding meaning in this life. You might ignore what I'm telling you. You might put this book down and carry on with your life like nothing has changed, but deep down you know I am right. You were made for so much more. You have so much to give. And, just like Solanus, the place where you work right now, in the heart of your family and in your vocation within Catholic education, is the exact place that God wants this to happen.

Sadly, popular culture seems to think that having a spiritual awakening requires a trip to Tibet or at the very least a yoga studio and ethically sourced coconut water. One of the great things about Catholicism is its sheer earthiness. While it has the sublime beauty of the Mass, it also recognizes the earthiness of its own symbols: bread, water and wine. The Incarnation itself is essentially scandalous. The supreme God of the universe entering human flesh and experiencing birth in a cattle stall full of the smells of the barn and the land. None of this is accidental. God loves us enough to know that it is through our everyday experiences that we can come to encounter Him. And this holds true for the way in which our work, our vocation, draws us to God, and, if we are open, to sainthood.

Reconnecting to Your Vocation

In Catholic thinking we have what's called a primary and secondary vocation. Your primary vocation can often be referred to as your "state of life." It's essentially being a single person, a married person or someone living religious life as a priest or brother or sister. While social media now offers over fifty-seven ways to define your identity, we only get three – but a little simplicity can be a good thing. Your secondary vocation is usually the work you take on in the world. It is the way you deploy your unique skills and abilities to pay the bills, find meaning, serve others and live your life.

The Catholic concept of vocation is an important one. We live in a culture that maximizes personal autonomy and gratification. Career choices are less made these days through the filter of vocation and meaning than they are through the filter of wealth and status. A few weeks ago I was shopping in my city and almost every shop clerk under the age of twenty-five was studying law. No offence, but do we really need that many lawyers? How many of those kids were saying in pre-school, "When I grow up, I want to be a lawyer!" Sure, be a lawyer by all means, if you love justice and care about it enough. And heck, you will probably own a Porsche eventually. Happy days!

My point here is that we need to reconnect to a much deeper sense of vocation both at the primary and secondary levels in our lives. What we need to understand is that God *uses* vocation to make us holy. That's the primary purpose of vocation. I've been married now for sixteen years and I always say to audiences that marriage will do one of two things. It will eventually make you a saint or it will kill you. It's definitely going to be one of those two things. Our vocations are the way in which God brings out our best gifts but also sandpapers off all the rough edges. This is a paradigm shift. Your state of life – your vocation – is really important. It's not, hopefully, some arbitrary choice you made on a whim. It's very, very significant. It's the primary way that God wants to make you holy.

My task in this book is not to fix your marriage or your priesthood. There are loads of books about that. I want to talk about your secondary vocation. I want to suggest that what you may have thought was a *job* is truly a vocation. Your role as a teacher or a principal or a janitor in a Catholic school is the way in which God is desperately trying to do two things. First, he is trying to use it to make you holy. He wants the joys and successes, the challenges and the failures and all the moments in between to be ways in which you both encounter Him and increasingly turn toward Him for help, healing, purpose, wisdom and creativity. Second, he wants to use your vocation to redeem the world. I'm serious. He wants to use your vocation to bind up the wounds of a broken humanity. He wants to use your vocation to help that kid no one believes in to keep going because God knows that kid could win the Nobel prize one day. And you know that teacher in your faculty you just can't stand? Yeah, that one! God wants you to grow in holiness so you can bring a word of kindness to them when they descend into another black fog of depression. He wants you to make disciples so that more young people can know they are loved eternally and that they have a hope and a purpose and a destiny. He wants you to help that quiet kid to understand the value and dignity of the human person because that kid is one day going to law school and then she's going to become Chief Justice of the Supreme Court and fight for a culture of life because of something you taught them fifty years earlier.

He has no hands but yours, no voice but yours. If not you, then who? Your vocation can make you a saint and heal the world. I mean that from my heart and I believe it in the core of my being and the rest of my life is dedicated to telling everyone who will listen that Catholic education matters because it makes saints and it heals the world and transforms culture.

You must never lose sight of this again. You have a vocation, you do *not* have a job. Vocation, of course, comes from the Latin *vocare,* which means to call forth or to draw out. Your vocation is how God is calling forth or drawing out the very best of what is deep within you. Becoming a saint will never, for a moment, diminish anything of your amazing natural giftedness. It will simply allow God to draw more of it out. People often fear that going more deeply into relationship with God will somehow kill off their natural interests and talents and they'll become boring and sit around praying rosaries all day. Nothing could be further from the truth. Vocation is all about drawing out and calling forth the very best of all you have for the world.

And, in a related sense, vocation is also how you call forth and draw out the very best of your students. In a consumerist and secular world that crushes them into narrow categories, God has placed you in their lives to uncover and call out their special giftedness. How many children have left our schools where no one – no teacher, no parent, no principal – saw their special gifts and those gifts withered into silence? Those students now sit in cubicles doing work they hate and their dreams will die with them. Saints would never let this happen, and even if you don't believe me yet, I believe that you're a saint in the making.

So how exactly are we going to become saints? Like this…

Dependence:

The state of relying on someone or something else.

Chapter 6

The Path of Dependence

Does your life ever feel complex? I am not sure whether it's a function of age but, man, does my life feel complex at times. I woke up this morning at 4 am. I was already late for a video conference call to Washington from here in Australia. I don't speak to humans in the morning without first ingesting half the caffeine production of a small South American nation. It was 4.17 by the time the call was about to start. By 5 am I left the house for a training ride. I did a brutal training ride with a bunch of elite cyclists through the beautiful streets of our national capital. Not that I noticed any of that beauty with my nose inches from the handlebars and my lungs trying to bilocate. Cafe stop. More caffeine ingestion. Home.

It's now 7.15 am. I enter into high-level negotiations with three children under eight in a heroic attempt to get them to school in some form of cleanliness so as not to be reported to the government. The United Nations Security Council has it easy when it comes to the negotiations, sanctions and threats I go through each morning. It's now 10 am and here I am, dear reader, about to wrap up this book.

So Much To Do, Such Little Time

Complexity. We start life with so little on our schedule and before we blink there are swimming classes, cello practice, soccer and interpretive dance classes. You may or may not remember the great, early promises of technology, but one of them was that it was going to give us loads of free time and leisure. How's that working for you so far? Pope Benedict made an interesting observation when he stated:

> *"...our technological society has succeeded in multiplying occasions of pleasure, yet has found it very difficult to engender joy."*

Complexity makes it hard to experience joy and to cut through to the core of what really matters in our vocations as Catholic educators. There just seems so much to *do* and so little time to do it. All this busyness makes it hard to focus upon the essential. Spend just a few moments on any major social platform that involves educators and you'll also see how the education vocation has been corporatized. So many of the leadership and management theories that emerge from Harvard Business Review soon enough end up being espoused in the education space. All of this is simply my way of suggesting that it can be hard to see our way through to the *how* of helping our schools, and for you, as an educator, to fulfill the mission of Catholic education.

The good news is that I do have some good news. The good news is that I think the answer is simple. Once again, it's not easy but it is simple, and so I want to make a simple point. The answer to all our challenges in Catholic education is not a system. It's not a new form of practice or some clever pedagogy or latest managerial technique. It does not require that you learn some new approach or paradigm or clever theory on human behavior. The very good news is simply this: the *way* is a *person.*

The Answer is Jesus

One of the reasons that St. Paul was so darn influential in human history was that he was, like Mary, one of the first people to really understand just what God was up to in human history. The Classical society into which he injected himself with such force wanted something very different to what he was presenting. The Greeks and Romans wanted wisdom, knowledge and insight. The Romans, particularly, had developed quite robust "systems for living." The stoicism of Marcus Aurelius's *Meditations* shows a highly developed metaphysical and philosophical approach to reality. As a culture they had got really good at trying to endure the slings and arrows of existence with as much cognitive protection as possible.

Hebrew culture had taken a different approach. Having seen the hand of God in action, they had soon enough become fixated with bowl-washing rituals and making sure enough lambs were queued up for High Priest's dinner each night. It's another very human response. Let's take the experience of God and His power to act in history, and reduce it to systems and protocols and a caste system of insiders and outsiders. What made Paul so profoundly transformative of the cultures he encountered was that he was playing a whole new game. He had experienced the inability of systems and ideologies to bring healing and encounter and transformation. He was among the very first people to discover the one central truth that can reform Catholic education, and that truth is that the *way is a person.*

The way to heal our schools and reach our students and live our mission is not a system. It's not a program. It's a person. You can forget anything else I tell you in this book, but you must not forget that. If the *person* of Jesus Christ becomes the firm foundation of all that we do and try to accomplish in our schools, then we are going to be fine. In fact, we are going to be better than fine. We are going to live our vocations with energy and impact and joy, and we won't burn out and descend into cynicism.

St. Paul understood this. Over and over again, when people wanted something else, he just presented them with a *person.* The person of Jesus. Think also of St. Peter in Acts 3:6. A beggar is asking for cash and Peter says, "Silver or gold I do not have, but what I do have I give you. In the name of Jesus Christ of Nazareth, walk." Peter did not respond to this very real human situation with a program or a philosophy. He responded with a person. For so long I think we have been building with the wrong foundation in Catholic schools. For so long we've been focusing solely on our tools but almost completely ignoring our fuels. We've been building upon our own cleverness, our credentials, our fear of not being seen to be churning out brilliant students and thereby disappointing parents and bishops and the news media. We've stopped building on the firm foundation of Jesus Christ and upon His power and His spirit and His boundless resources, which can transform us and change our schools. The real question is simply how much longer we'd like to continue in our foolishness.

My father used to have this saying that he picked up somewhere: "I don't know what the question is, but I am sure the answer is Jesus." Whatever questions and challenges we face in Catholic education, I truly believe that they can be both understood and overcome by a radical new relationship with and dependence upon the very real person of Jesus Christ.

Dependence on Him

My daughter has some challenges at her school. Nothing dramatic, just normal stuff – fitting in, negotiating friendships, that sort of stuff. I sat on her bed the other night and shared something that I have learned at very great cost over many years. I asked her that if Jesus could speak the entire cosmos into existence and sustain it in each millisecond by His own sovereign decree, did she think it may, hypothetically, be possible that He could help with her circumstance? There was a long pause and she agreed that it was just possible that the supreme creative force of the entire universe, of all that is seen and unseen, might just be able to help transform either her or her circumstance.

My friend, our problem in Catholic education is not that God is absent. The problem is that we've indirectly asked Him to leave. We've reduced the power that flowed through Paul and Peter to a nativity play once per year and a mission statement that no one reads. Our problem in Catholic education is simply that we expect too much of ourselves and virtually nothing of God. I know this is true the same way I know the sun will rise tomorrow. It's visceral for me. It's seeped into my bones after so many years being a mute witness to the failure of our schools to live up to their high calling. In my early years of teaching I accepted the patronizing suggestions that I was too keen or too energetic or too idealistic. Over time, I began to wonder if maybe it wasn't me. Maybe the system itself was broken? Maybe the mission had been missed? One more time: we expect too much of ourselves and way too little of Jesus and His very real power and presence. The way is a person.

This is my bedrock position. It's what I have been calling the *path of dependence.* We have to let go of our plans and agendas and pride and systems and micro-management and abandon ourselves to a new and deeper relationship with Jesus. It is this and this alone that will transform our schools. When saints walk the corridors, schools change. It's that simple. And to become saints, as I have already said, we must set our feet, today, upon the path of dependence.

More than anyone I know, I tried to win at life and at teaching by sheer grunt and muscle. I pushed myself so hard for so many years and I just ended up with an anxiety disorder and depression. I constructed a life based around *my* performance which made me exquisitely vulnerable to people's approval and opinions of me. If *I* was teaching well then I was safe. If I was being noticed then I was OK. I relied on me. It was utterly exhausting and completely unsustainable. I think that many of us carry a deep wound in our lives about our own worth and ability. We find the idea of unconditional love basically impossible to believe. Most of us have never really experienced it so we can't even imagine a God that could see us through that lens. The result is that we find some small area of our life or work that we *can* be valued for and then we often end up building an entire identity around that. I know that early in my teaching career I came to merge my success with students into the core of my sense of self at that time. When that happens you also have to live with the fear that you must keep it all working. You're only as good as your last class or the approval and validation of your principal, your students or their parents. It's a precarious way to live.

As a result of living that life and the pain that came with it I feel I can save you so much wasted time and energy. I've been down the path of self-reliance and I don't want to go there ever again. That way lies madness. Why do you think we have such a self-medicating and therapeutic- and entertainment-obsessed culture? It's because we think we're alone and it scares the hell out of us. We are not alone. You are not alone. There are great and mighty arms to carry us if we'll just stop struggling in our own strength and let ourselves be carried. All the saints came to this. ALL OF THEM. Why do you think St. Paul wanted us to understand that he had come to see all his achievements and glory as nothing but rubbish? Why? Simply because he had encountered Christ and he knew that was all he was ever going to need. I wish I had known that when I was a young teacher. I wish I had known that it was not up to me. I wish I had colleagues around me who were saints who could have mentored and guided me into understanding that the God who had called me into teaching was the same God who could sustain me in teaching. I had to learn all this slowly and painfully. I guess the good news is that none of it was wasted if I can share it with you.

Do not be afraid. This path of dependence does not mean you stop being professional. It does not mean you stop using systems and programs. It just means that you no longer look to them to be *the* answer. You suddenly can breathe again because it's no longer your problem to fix. Your only real task is dependence. Jesus will become the sustaining presence that carries you. He becomes your wisdom when you don't know what choice to make. He supernaturally imparts patience when you have no patience. He gifts you charity when you genuinely dislike someone. He inspires you with a hunger for truth, beauty and goodness that changes how and what you teach and why you teach it. If Jesus is not in the business of changing and transforming people, then Paul's words that we are dead in our sins and deserving of pity are true. They are not true.

So, here endeth the lesson! Are you with me? I am only saying *one* thing. Dependence. That's it. Will you surrender your life and your agenda and your plans and your fleeting power in this world to Jesus Christ or will you not? If you have done so, then will you go deeper? Will you seek Him more earnestly and surrender more fully? Scripture is very clear that every knee is going to bow and every tongue is going to confess his Lordship. So you can do it now or you can do it in the next life, but you are going to do it. What's the upside of resisting this? What do we gain from enthroning our pale abilities at the center of our world? There is a whole new life waiting for you. A deeper life. A peace and a sense of being carried that I find so hard to explain. I just know that I gave up fighting. I made myself a mess for years and I really want to spare you that pain. Just give yourself to Him fully. He will make you into the teacher or leader or priest or principal or bishop that only He knows you can be. I thought I was going to be a fighter pilot or a spy. The life I have found in Him has been incredible. It is only in hindsight I can see the richness and fullness of the life I found in Him. He knew what I was best at and brought me there despite all my time-wasting and doubt. Trust me, you have no idea what He has in store for you and how He will use you unless you just let go and place your feet, today, upon the path of dependence.

So, how do you do that?

The Sacraments

Sometimes I tell people that I used to drink professionally for Australia. There was a time, earlier in my life, when I grew exceedingly fond of alcohol. In my late teens I ended up on the other side of the world in a very fancy boarding school helping out with rugby coaching. When not working, I could be found in the local pub along with other guys my age on the staff. I console myself these years later with the thought that quite a few saints often spent their formative years in bars. Marcellin Champagnat failed seminary more than once because he was usually skipping class and enjoying ale and Beaujolais with the local villagers.

During the year I spent coaching, I think I was having some kind of Jekyll and Hyde experience. While seeking to do my home nation, with its background of convicts and booze hounds, proud, I also started attending daily Mass. It was a Jesuit school and not only was there daily mass, there was daily Mass in a five hundred-year-old chapel. There is something about five hundred-year-old chapels that puts you in perspective. It's a bit like how you feel at Niagara Falls. You get a sense of your place in the scheme of things. In a five hundred-year-old chapel you realize that vast numbers of people have come to this same room to seek...*something.* I remember, all these years later, standing in that room and each day the same words of the liturgy kept seeming to impress themselves with unusual force into my consciousness: "...the blood of the new and everlasting covenant that will be shed for you and for many." Drinking like I did, I had no problem understanding I was a heinous sinner on my way to perdition, but before I got there, I was struck with wondering why someone would want to shed their blood over it. It was not just those words, it was something else. It was not just the chapel, it was something else. Why did I keep coming?

As I write these words, it's 11.37 am on a Wednesday. In thirteen minutes' time, I am going to get into my car and drive across town to another small chapel. This one is not five hundred years old and it's not beautiful. In fact, when I come to power, the architect will be shot at dawn. But despite the green carpet, deplorable artwork and bad lighting, I need to be there. Why? Because both the teaching of the Church and forty-three years of experience have taught me that Jesus Christ is in His Church and in the sacraments of His Church. Joan of Arc said it nicely shortly before heading to the stake:

> *"About Jesus Christ and the Church, I simply know they're just one thing, and we shouldn't* ***complicate the matter.****"*

Jesus Christ and his Church are one. And the sacraments of the Church are the most powerful way in which we experience the real and living presence of Jesus. As Joan says, let's not make it complicated. We need to get this point. The sacraments of the Church are the main way – or in Church lingo we could say they are the most *efficacious* way – in which the power and presence and healing and wisdom of God are made manifest and real and tangible in our very real and physical world. So my point is this: if the sacraments are the main way in which the power of Jesus is made present, what happens when many teachers either do not understand what's on offer or don't make it a priority or both?

First, understand grace. Grace is the unmerited love and favor of God. I love that word *unmerited.* He gives grace not based on *anything* we've done or could do. It's what some people call the *scandal of grace.* As I discussed previously, in our human systems we award people based on what they do or how they look or where they fit in hierarchies. God is so unlike us in this sense it is amazing. God gives grace because He is God. It's what He does. I once spoke at a conference at a beach resort and I made the point that the tide cannot help but come in and go out. The tide does not change its behavior based upon how it feels or whether the coastline is its preferred coastline. It's the tide. It simply *does* what it *is.* Ever noticed that the Bible tells us that Jesus Christ is the same yesterday, today and forever? He will not give grace today and stop next Tuesday at 4 pm if you tell a lie or cheat on your taxes. He will keep giving grace.

Through the sacraments God gives grace. Through the sacraments God changes you via that same grace. He may change your circumstance. He may change the actual issues you pray to Him about, but more often He just changes you. He gives you the capacity to cope with or transcend or be different, maybe holier, than you would otherwise have been. So my premise is that if God is trying to give us grace through the sacraments but many of us are either not attending the sacraments or in some way closed off to the grace of those sacraments, then would that not explain part of the reason that our schools have failed to achieve their mission? It's not like God withheld grace. We just stopped positioning ourselves to receive it. My evangelical Protestant friends often talk about *positioning* themselves in God's house or *positioning* themselves for a new outpouring of God's spirit. Whatever our doctrinal differences, I admire the seriousness with which they take this need to be in a place to receive the grace that God always wants to give.

What I am saying is that if we want to renew Catholic education, if you want to become the teacher you were made to become, then I can promise you this will not happen without a regular encounter with Jesus in the sacraments. For years I have done seminars for teachers where I point them to a simple line in the catechism that tells us that the Eucharist is the *"source and summit of the faith."* Read those words again slowly: *source and summit.* According to Church teaching, the Eucharist is both the source from which flows our entire Catholic faith and it is also the peak, the summit, the pinnacle of what it means to encounter Jesus as a Catholic. Look around you. You may be an exception, but how many Catholics do you know, how many teachers do you know, who have re-oriented their life around this truth? If the Eucharist is this important, and if it is not taken seriously by so many Catholics and, for our purpose, so many teachers who are Catholic, then might that not be one good reason that our schools are struggling?

In the Old Testament there is a constant call to repentance, to turning back. I deeply feel that we need to call each other back to the sacraments. We need to become a teaching profession of people deeply purged of self-reliance and deeply immersed in reliance upon the real presence of Jesus in the Eucharist. Can you think of any saints who were indifferent to the Eucharist? Why did Mother Teresa insist her nuns spend two hours each day in Eucharistic adoration? What did she want her sisters to understand? Surrounded by all that need why did she not cut it to thirty minutes and let them do an extra ninety minutes per day of ministry? It was because she knew better than anyone what it takes to sustain a ministry. It takes Jesus, and Jesus is in the sacraments. Think of the woman in the Gospel who broke the jar of perfume and wiped Jesus's feet with her tears. She was chastised for not selling the perfume and giving the money away. People wanted her to be practical, she just wanted to worship. It was that worship of Jesus that utterly changed her life. What do you think is happening in Eucharistic adoration? What do you think is happening in the Mass? It's the same Jesus she wept over, but we no longer know how to have our hearts broken by His presence. We need to turn back and seek Him while He is still to be found, and you *can* find Him in the sacraments.

Do I always hear choirs of angels sing every time I go to Mass? No. Do I always feel transformed after I receive the Eucharist? No. But what I do know is that it is simply my role to turn up, to be present, to be hungry. I can't really explain what happens. It's just that over the years I have a deeper and deeper love for the Mass and the Eucharist. I am not some retrograde arch-conservative. I ride a Harley and when I kick my toe or hit myself with a hammer I swear like a sailor. But then I go to confession. My point is that I am normal. If you passed me on the street, apart from recognizing my boyish charm and good looks, I'd be unremarkable. I say this because there seems to be a sense that if you take the sacraments seriously, then you must be joyless or repressed or both.

I'm neither. What I do know is an increasing sense of dependence, an increasing desire to simply find Christ in the sacraments and allow His grace to slowly bring about His purposes for my life.

My point in all this is simply that the renewal of Catholic education is going to come about through saints. Saints like you. And one thing we know about all the saints is that they wanted to be with Jesus. If Jesus is present in the sacraments, then you just need to be where the sacraments are. It's that simple.

For a long time in my life I would get up at 4 am and drive to a small chapel that had Eucharistic adoration. I would spend an hour each morning on my knees in those still small hours. I had this joke in my seminars where I would really build this up. I would set the scene and explain to the audience how I had got up so early and driven so far and spent several years in front of the Blessed Sacrament. I would build up the intensity of this scene and then I would say, "And after years of this, do you know what God said to me?" The audience would be hushed and would lean in toward me ever so slightly. I would pause and then say, "Nothing! In two years of going pretty much every day, I never heard a thing."

My point was that I did not go there to get hot tips for sporting events or beatific visions. I went there because I knew I was not able to make my life "work" on my own and that one of the only things I *did* know was that I wanted more of His presence and Lordship in my life. It just seems that God won't trust you with too much until He knows you don't need it. In three weeks from now I will be launching this book at a conference where I am doing the keynote for almost ten thousand people. There was a time in my life when I would have been paralyzed by this. Why? Because I would have been desperate to get it right, to be perfect. I would have been desperate to make people think I was clever and talented. My whole identity and sense of worth would have been hinging on how I performed. Now I just want Jesus. If He puts me on stage in front of ten thousand or fifty thousand or a stadium of a hundred thousand, that's fine. If I never speak again to any audience, that's fine. I just want to know Him and He is in the sacraments and the sacraments are in His Church.

You have to understand that you are never going to be the teacher He created you to be without a greater dependence upon Him and upon His grace. Please, I beg you, make time for the sacraments. Re-orient your life to get to Mass as often as you can. Go to confession. Why? Is it because you're a vile sinner in risk of sulfur and brimstone? No. It's because all of us are wounded, broken people, and wounded, broken people cause havoc in their pain if they don't get healed. Jesus is present in the sacrament of confession. He is the healer. We go to confession so we can be healed. When we are more healed and whole, we can love more. Great teachers are humble, broken, healed people. The sacrament of confession leads you to love God more because, over time, you see Him slowly work with your broken patterns and compulsions and addictions. The prodigal son was loved, not for anything he did. He was loved because he was the son of a father and he made one smart move and only one: he came home. Confession *is* coming home, but these days it's like we all want to live as prodigals and stay on the farm eating swill. Come home. Be healed. Then you can love more fully.

Prayer

I refuse to be daunted by the fact that vast numbers of people significantly holier and smarter than me have written countless volumes on prayer. I'll make my contribution pretty simply. I remember learning in my post-grad program about two simple ideas that can help us understand prayer. The first was the Latin term *capax dei*. It simply means "the capacity for God." The human person can be referred to as possessing this attribute. We are the sort of *thing* that has the capacity for God. Considering the large number of unhinged people who seem to think animals are like humans but just can't talk, let's remind ourselves of something. There is a vast gulf between the human person as the pinnacle of creation and your beloved Labrador or goldfish. While I accept we can't conclusively rule this out, animals do not relate to God in the way that we do. Aristotle would say that they do relate to God simply by being fully what God created them to be. For example, a goldfish relates to God by giving God glory in that it is being exactly what God created it to be. It fulfills its divine purpose. However, as I mentioned before, I went to daily Eucharistic adoration for years and I never once shared a pew with a Labrador. The Labrador is not *capax dei*. I am.

The second simple idea is that we are *contingent beings*. We did not create ourselves. Our existence comes *from* something, *someone*, else. Our existence is contingent upon the existence of God. The Genesis story talks of God shaping man from the dust of the earth and breathing the breath of life into his nostrils. We did not shape ourselves from the preternatural clay and we did not breathe life into our own beings. We are dependent. If God withdrew His presence, His spirit, His breath of life from us, we would cease to exist in a nanosecond.

When you put these two great realities together, you get what I call a *fundamental disposition*. We have both the capacity *for* God and are truly dependent *upon* God. Our fundamental disposition, our orientation toward God should come from these two realities. We need God because of what we *are*. The nature of being human creates the necessity for prayer. I want to suggest that to be an authentic Catholic teacher, to fulfill your vocation, cries out for a return to prayer. This, of course, begs the question, what is prayer?

Best I can tell, prayer is simply the expression of a hunger to be *with* God. I don't pray because I am scared of God, I pray because I am scared of me! I am scared of what happens when I try to be a husband or father without a dependence upon God. Prayer is the expression of that need. But it's also more than that. To make prayer just an expression of dependence can lead to a kind of spiritual utilitarianism. We must not *use* God to try to make our life work. Prayer is simply the desire to be *with* God, however that is expressed by each person in their journey of relationship with God.

Also, it's worth remembering that heaven will be the ultimate consummation of that desire. The joy of heaven will simply be that we will finally be with God. The fundamental disposition of what it means to be human will be fulfilled in its unutterable totality. Prayer is prefiguring here and now what will be our ultimate and inexpressible joy there.

OK, so this all sounds a bit esoteric, a bit fancy. How does prayer relate to the real Catholic teacher in a real school with challenging kids, limited resources and increasing demands? I think it ties in with my core narrative about the path of dependence and the centrality of Jesus. Prayer is the cry of the Catholic teacher at the start of each day, "Lord, help me today, please guide me, sustain me and inspire me." It's the recognition of dependence and need and hope. It's the recognition that the needs of our time, the pressures of our culture, the wellbeing of our young people are so far beyond our own limited capacity that we need the hand of God upon each school day and each class and each hour and each conversation.

From my experience there is some kind of vast paradox at work here. We are both highly capable and simultaneously incapable. We are educational professionals but each day we begin again and seek to learn how to love, how to be patient, how to listen. God knows we have gifts and that there is much we can do, but he wants to elevate those gifts. The tragedy is that through busy-ness, secularism, exhaustion and more, so many Catholic teachers have stopped asking Him for help. Prayer is asking for help. If you've had children, do you remember when they were little and they needed something from you? Those soft hands and those little voices. Even when you were tired you stopped what you were doing and met their needs. Newsflash! God never gets tired. He is always present. He knows what we need before we ask, but we do have to ask.

In about half an hour my three little kids will get home from school. They will be tired, hungry and wanting to rest and eat. I don't say, "Take a number and I'll get to you later." I stop what I'm doing and try to be attentive to their needs. God is like that with all the needs you have, but infinitely more attentive and capable. We just need to re-learn how to ask.

So, please, begin to pray again. Just stop in at your school chapel or make time at home. Whatever it takes. Become a person of prayer. You don't have to tell the world, wear hair shirts or kneel in the snow for hours. You can just make time to be with the God who is desperate to be with you. There is a wonderful line in the Second Book of Chronicles where God says:

> *"If my people, which are called by my name, shall humble themselves, and pray, and seek my face, and turn from their wicked ways; then will I hear from heaven, and will forgive their sin, and will heal their land."*

It can't get much clearer than that and there is not much difference between the times the Israelites were living in and our own. If enough Catholic teachers will turn and humble themselves and seek God's face and begin to pray, then God will hear from heaven, forgive them their sins, heal them and then heal their classrooms and their whole schools. I wish I could give you some clever mantra or system or plan, but I just don't have one. I have Jesus and I have the sacraments and I have prayer, and if you make those three things central in your life then you will achieve and experience so much more than any plan or system could ever offer.

Scripture

A final strategy that we need to begin to open to is a greater role for sacred Scripture in our lives. Buried deep within our Catholic psyche is the intractable idea that Scripture is something that we hear once a week. We may or may not pay attention to the homily and that's pretty much it. We know that our Protestant friends are pretty serious about it but, for most of us, it's not something that really occupies too much of our lives. This has really begun to change for me in recent times. And I want to thank Joyce Meyer!

Oh, heresy of heresies! Here I am, a Catholic, writing a very Catholic book for Catholic teachers and I just mentioned Joyce Meyer! I can't help it, I just really like her. I like her because she is authentic and she is another great example of God using the most unlikely people to do the most amazing things. She talks about her abusive childhood, her temper and all the other reasons that God should have chosen someone else, anyone else, to do the work she does. I don't want you to like Joyce Meyer if you really don't like her. That's not my point. We all have different preferences.

However, one of the things Joyce Meyer does well is point us to the raw power of the Bible to help us see reality correctly. After the fall of Adam and Eve, one of the consequences is that we simply don't see the world, the universe, each other and God the way we were created to. Our spiritual capacity to see things as they truly are has been skewed, sometimes badly. Apart from our wounded spiritual selves, there is also our personal psychology and all the baggage we bring from our past. As such, we often see people, situations and life in general with some degree of what I'm going to call *problematic inaccuracy.*

The Bible, among many other things, helps us to see the world and each other as it really is. Importantly, it's not simply a case of the *words* of the Bible helping us to have *better ideas.* We could get that from any self-help book. It's not a case of the Bible helping us to win friends and influence people or making us nicer. The Bible, and the God who is speaking through it, is not asking us to consider its words as nice advice that we should take away and consider. The Bible operates on a completely different level. The Bible has *power.* It possesses a supernatural capacity to change our lives because the Holy Spirit both inspired it and is still speaking through it. Every moment, every day, all of our lives. So let's be very clear: the Bible is not a collection of nice sentiments we can frame in our mission statements, though sadly that's about as close to deploying the power of Scripture as some schools will ever get.

As a Catholic teacher, making more time to sit with sacred Scripture is going to do at least two main things if not many more. First, it is going to help you to see correctly. It's going to help you to see yourself, your vocation and your moment in history much more clearly. It's going to reveal to you the truth that you are, in fact, caught up in a vast cosmic battle between the God who claims every square inch of the universe and the diabolical forces that counterclaim it. It's going to help you see that every single student, parent and member of staff in your school community was made in the image and likeness of God, and that the call is upon your life and behavior to recognize that and respond accordingly, even when it is very hard to do so.

As you learn to see correctly you will more deeply discover the deeply mysterious, wonderful, subversive, confronting, confusing and magnificent character of Jesus. You will find Him more and more someone you could give your life to. In fact, I stood in a church the other day staring at a brilliantly shaped crucifix depicting a deeply inspiring Christ. I said to someone with me, "You know, I have never been one of those 'ooh, Jesus, I love you so much' types, but I would follow that man through the gates of hell." The Jesus I found in the Gospels is a deeply compelling figure I have come to learn can be trusted with my entire life and its purpose and plan.

Scripture will change you. You will come to see differently. Think of that one student you really don't like. In our fallen human state we find so many viable ways to convince ourselves of just how deplorable that student is. We resent them and we come to dislike the very sight of their insolence, disrespect and disregard for us. Scripture then deploys the most inconvenient of truths in that it tells us that God not only created that student but loves them so intensely that He suffered and died for them. Then, as we begin to complain and moan about how this one student must be the exception to the entire Gospel, Jesus tells us to pick up our cross and follow Him. He tells us that we will have trouble in this life but not to fear because He has conquered the world. Over and over again, the Bible will challenge our terrible eyesight and confront us with a more expansive and noble vision of our high calling in Jesus. It will not only show us that vision – it will mysteriously give us a growing, gradual power to live it.

Robert Frost once wrote that "a man is what he thinks about all day long." Our exposure to Scripture over time begins to shape how we see and how we love and what we choose and what we say and how we seek forgiveness and how we surrender our pride. In short, as Frost understood, it is the dominant thoughts of our hearts and minds that shape our interaction with the world and with other people. As we immerse ourselves in the story of Scripture, we truly begin to live differently.

On a practical level, you just need to start small. I have a simple program on my phone that gives me my daily readings. Each morning, at some ungodly hour, I get out my journal and my Bible and go through the readings. I write down key lines, I underline others. And then I do it again. Day after day after day. I am often tired but I know it matters. It matters for the one great reason that it is another way that I open myself to the presence of grace and the God who wants to reveal Himself to me so that I can live my vocation fully, love my family and, in some small way, serve the needs of the world. And, to be honest, there are some moments, not many, when God has spoken to me so directly and powerfully through His word in Scripture that I have been literally speechless.

Once I was dealing with a very great decision. I was afraid and that fear was crippling me. I had to make a choice within twenty-four hours and it was a major turning point in my life. I found myself back on my knees again before the Blessed Sacrament. I was desperate. Eventually, immersed deeply in my Bible, I came across a Scripture I had never read before. I had read my Bible for many years, but I had never seen this. It was an obscure verse hidden deep in the Old Testament. It spoke so directly into my circumstance I literally looked around the empty church to see if someone was maybe filming me or if this was some kind of bizarre practical joke. I cannot remember in my entire life being so impacted by a verse of the Bible answering the deepest questions of my heart. I sat in a stunned silence for a long time and then made ready to leave the church. As I was locking the door, I received a message on my phone from Karen. She said she had been praying for me and had found a verse in the Bible she wanted to share with me. It was the *same* verse.

I know the skeptic among us would talk of coincidence. Later I did a quick check and learned that there are over 54,000 individual verses in the Bible. What is the statistical likelihood that two people in separate locations, at exactly the same time, would both find the same verse that neither had ever seen before among *54,000* possible verses? Either way, that verse answered my question. I made my choice. My decision eventually led to reaching more and more people around the world and changing the course of my life. I know in the depth of my heart that the Holy Spirit used the Bible to direct my life. So ask yourself: why should you be any different?

Please make this a priority. Please make some time *every* day of your life to be with God in the sacred Scripture. St Jerome said that ignorance of Scripture is ignorance of God. He is in there. Jesus is the Word of God. The Spirit is speaking through those pages. You will never be the teacher you have been created to be without coming to spend time with Him in those pages. Just make it five minutes per day. Before you start your day, stop into the school chapel and sit in the stillness. Open a Bible and ask the Holy Spirit to speak to your heart. Maybe follow the readings of the day, maybe do some other form of guided reflection. My friend, I don't care if you hang from the roof reading the Bible in the original Greek, as long as you are reading the Bible. Don't let another day go by as a Catholic teacher without committing to becoming a man or woman of Scripture.

If you're a principal or have some leadership role in Catholic education, it's even more important. You cannot be the shepherd God has called you to be without Scripture. How can you grow in wisdom and discernment without His words in your heart, mind and mouth? We don't really need more MBAs. They can be helpful if that is your charism and it helps you to better discharge your vocation. What we really need is more saints, and the saints found God in the Bible and so can you.

One Belief, Three Strategies

So there is one belief and three strategies that every Catholic educator *must* manifest in their lives to become all they are capable of becoming. The stakes are high. Young people and our entire world urgently need your best.

The belief is that we must seek the path of dependence. We must let go of all our cleverness and self-reliance and radically seek the face of the risen Christ. It is only in Him, in deep, daily relationship with Him, that we can ever hope to bind up the wounds of the broken hearted, open the eyes of the blind and truly declare a season of the Lord's favor. We cannot do this any more in our own strength. It is the fast track to despair, burnout, cynicism and exhaustion.

The first strategy for achieving this is that we *must* seek the grace of God that flows like a torrent through the sacraments. Christ is in the sacraments and the sacraments are in His church. Please make frequent communion a priority, not because you are going to become all pious and super-spiritual. Do it for the same reason that the woman soaked Jesus's feet in tears. Do it just to be *with* Him, because that is what you were made for and it will bring you healing and peace. And from that healing and peace, you will be ever more a blessing for others. Seek also the grace of confession. Bring your wounds and your sin to the very presence of Jesus Himself in the person of the priest. Frequent confession will help you become a saint.

The second strategy is to become a person of prayer. However the Lord leads, you just give Him time. We live in a hectic and crazy world and the saints of tomorrow will be people of silence and stillness and contemplation who drink from deep wells of grace. Do not start any day of teaching without surrendering your life and vocation to Him. Humble yourself and cry out for His grace and favor and inspiration and presence in your life. Pray for your students, especially the ones you like the least. Pray for your fellow teachers, especially the ones you like the least. You don't have to be fancy. Just sit at the feet of Jesus and be with Him, but don't spend another day of your life trying to do this journey of life and the vocation of teaching without casting yourself upon Him each day.

The third strategy is to become a person of Scripture. You don't have to attend the Biblicum in Rome or translate Aramaic. You just have to pull out your phone and look up the readings for the day and then make a small amount of time to sit with them. Ask the Holy Spirit to inspire you before you start. Allow the words to become written on your heart as the days, weeks and years roll by. In time, you will become what you think about all day.

A Final Word

My father's grave is unremarkable. On the few occasions I've been there, it always takes me a while to find it. I remember being there the day he was lowered into the earth, but it's still hard to find. My father remains a mystery to me. After all this time, still a mystery. As some of you will know, it is a poignant human experience to grow older and wonder what your parents might have been experiencing at the age you've reached. I am now a father and can filter my conflicts and rejection of him through the lens of my own imperfect parenting skills. Time, it seems, makes us kinder judges. One thing I do know about my father, however, is that he lived his life essentially hating every moment of his working life. I want to spare you from making the same mistake.

When my father was sixteen, my grandfather dropped dead in front of him. A week later he was sent to boarding school where he was brutalized mercilessly for years. He patched together a life of sorts but never overcame the depression and self-loathing that crippled him permanently. He had come from a family that had done extremely well in the post-war reconstruction boom of the 1950s. He was soon forced into the family building firm and hated it his entire life. His life taught me one great single lesson. Hating what you do for work is a terrible way to live. It broke his spirit and he never recovered.

I understand that many good men and women over the scope of human history have done work they hated to allow their families to survive. There is a quiet and deeply dignified heroism in this. In our culture of self-absorption their sacrifice seems bizarre, but that says much more about us than it does about them. However, it is unlikely, at least in the developed world, that you will have to do work you truly hate.

So, I want to leave you with a final thought. I believe that if you've read this far, there is a very good chance that God has called you into what I've been calling for years the *great adventure of Catholic education*. I believe you have a vocation. I believe that what you thought was a *job,* or maybe just enjoying working with young people, is so much more than that. I believe that you are partnering with God in reaching the lost and changing the world. I believe that your life as an educator has meaning, significance, value and purpose. I also think that when you are deeply living that vocation, when you are deeply connected to the channels of grace flowing through the heart of the Church, then you are putting a smile on God's face. Remember how I mentioned that as a parent you are rarely happier than when you see your kids happy and thriving in the things that leverage their gifts and bring them joy?

My father's life taught me that great sadness and suffering comes from the suppression of your gifts. It's a slow death when you can't bring your gifts to the world. You die on the inside and the world is impoverished and never gets to experience all that you could have done. You *are* a Catholic educator. This is what you *are.* This is your truth. And if you love this vocation, I desperately don't want to see you burn out and quit. You have so much left to do. There are so many students you have yet to reach. The Church needs your vocation. The world needs your vocation. It's time to be deeply proud of what you do and it's time to deeply connect yourself to the sources of renewal that will sustain you over the long haul.

In time, as you surrender and set your feet upon the path of dependence, as you seek the sacraments, as you pray and read Scripture, your vocation will deepen. In time you will become an ever-deeper image of the One who called you and sent you among the young and the lost and the broken. In time you will master your art and you will be one of those special teachers we've all known over the years. You will be one of those teachers who saw in a child what they could not see in themselves and you will call that to life. And one day you will open your eyes and hear a voice you know better than your own and it will say, "Well done, good and faithful servant, come and enter into your master's happiness." And I will see you there.